BREAK THE CYCLE

Lose Weight and Maintain Your Weight for the Rest of Your Life

BY

Karen Warwick, RHN

Disclaimer:

This book is not a substitute for medical advice and should not be taken as such. Please consult with a medical professional before making any diet or lifestyle changes.

Client Testimonials
(First Names Only to Reserve Confidentiality)

I have just completed my 3-month Jump Start package. I have lost 12 pounds; my skin is healthier and I feel better. I am more confident and happier because I am healthier. If you stick to Karen's plan, you will see results. My doctor said, 'Keep doing what you're doing.' Thank you, Karen, for your caring and professionalism.

Terry H.

I would absolutely recommend Karen. My stress levels are down, I lost 28 pounds and have more energy. Karen is truly a kind, caring person who wants to help individuals achieve their goals. I am proof of that! She sits down and takes the time with you. If you listen to what she has to say and do the work, you will get results.

Kevin S.

Before starting the program, I was struggling with my weight, diabetes and acid reflux. I have lost 12 pounds effortlessly, and have been able to reduce my medication for both diabetes and acid reflux. I have increased energy, a positive mood and greater focus. This program is life changing. Thank you so much Karen for improving my overall health!

Lenny H.

Thank you for kick starting my health and fitness in the right direction for my personal future. Before my consultation with you I knew I needed to do something but was unsure how to start and the direction I needed to take. Now I feel I have a plan and each day I feel I'm closer to my nutrition plan goals.

Cheryl B.

Karen, my one-on-one with you gave me clarity on which direction my diet needed to change to make me feel better for now and my future. When you don't have the help, it feels bleak and overwhelming on how to change. Thank you for the tools to do this. P.S. Special thanks for your recommendation of 'bromelain' for my arthritic knees. It really helped with the pain.

Tim B.

I was on the internet searching for nutritional 'experts' to glean ideas for diet, weight loss and quite frankly, better wellbeing as I felt tired a lot of the time. I assumed this was because I was over 65 and age was catching up on me. As well, I was really concerned about cholesterol, both good and bad, as I am taking various pills to reduce the all-important numbers that my doctor reviews with disgust every 6 months when they are posted. All of this has changed for the good and my doctor said recently, ' whatever you are doing keep doing it because it is working'. I left feeling really great about myself.

Through V.I. Holistic Nutrition and especially Karen, I have learned to identify issues, understand which foods have bad cholesterol, recognize sugar intake (hidden in foods) and as a result have lost 15kgs (33 pounds) slowly over 10 months (because I didn't want this to be a diet thing, I wanted this to be a change in lifestyle) and have maintained that level for the past 2 months even while travelling overseas. Now that my low cholesterol numbers and weight have stabilized, I will gently take on my next goal of losing another 10kgs through healthy eating and understanding my nutritional needs.

It has been an interesting journey from long distance and Karen has been extremely knowledgeable and helpful in my personal quest. I would recommend her and the company to all.

Glenn H.

Dedication

This book is dedicated to the two most important men in my life. To my dad, who has always been my role model and who, after a heart attack, changed his lifestyle to save his life. And to my husband, who always has my back and fills my days with love and laughter.

Your Free Gifts

As a way of saying thank you for purchasing this book, I provide support in my private Facebook group just for you. As a community we can share ideas, discuss our challenges and celebrate our victories.

Click here to join BREAK THE CYCLE: Lose Weight and Maintain Your Weight for Life

www.facebook.com/groups/1161831294241265

Also, I have given you a link to the Break the Cycle website where you can download the blank templates for free.

Click here to join: www.karenwarwickrhn.com

Table of Contents

INTRODUCTION

Here's a shocking fact for you. 70% of adult North Americans are either overweight or obese. Sadly, it is our new normal. How is this even possible with so many diet foods and weight loss programs available? We should all be super slim and living our best lives. Are we weak? Do we not have enough will power? No, that's not it. All weight loss programs tell amazing success stories. Their clients lose great amounts of weight in a short period of time. That shows amazing self control and discipline.

The problem is that diets are unsustainable. There are tedious amounts of weighing and measuring of food at every meal. You are almost chained to a kitchen scale. No one wants to spend the rest of their lives doing that. Or you are successful and lose the weight and then return to eating the Standard American Diet. Then the scale starts to creep back up again to the number that you started at or even higher!

Here's another fact for you. 70% of the North American diet is made up of processed foods. Can you see the correlation? These foods are loaded with sugar, fat and salt to make them especially delicious. And of course, make you especially fat. Every day you are eating far more calories than your body needs.

The extra is stored as fat. So, for health reasons our 'normal' diet is also unsustainable. You get so fat and frustrated with your weight that you find another weight loss program to try.

This is the cycle of yo-yo dieting. You put on fat by eating processed foods. Then, you go on a calorie restrictive diet and exercise like a fiend and lose the weight. You feel fantastic but you are starving. You start eating 'normally', and all the weight you lost comes back. Again, and again. Albert Einstein said that it was the definition of insanity. To do the same thing over and over and expect different results. This can also be the definition of yo-yo dieting.

I have found a way to break this cycle. It's not a new way. In fact, it's an old way. But I'll get into that in the book.

So, who is this book for?

You are in the right place if you have successfully lost weight on a diet only to regain the weight and then some. You are REALLY in the right place if you have done this more than once in your lifetime. This book is for you if you have problems with binge eating and/or night eating (cramming). It's for you if you are a fat vegan. It's for you if you are tired of weigh-and-measure diets. Or you are tired of diets with complicated recipes that need you to cook three meals a day every day. It's for you if you are tired of always thinking about food whether or not you are eating it. It's for you if you don't have a clue what makes up a health promoting diet. It's for you if you need a step-by-step method to start you off on a new healthy lifestyle.

This book is also for you if you are worried that your weight and eating habits are affecting your health. It's definitely for you if you have any of the big three of metabolic syndrome. Type 2 diabetes, heart disease and/or hypertension. It's for you if you have been prescribed medication to manage high blood sugar or high cholesterol. It's also for you if you have aches, pains or anything ending in -itis. It's for you if you lack energy. It's for you if you have low self esteem related to your ability to lose the weight and keep it off.

This program will give you the freedom that you have been seeking. Freedom from excess fat. Freedom from health worries. And freedom from guilt and self loathing.

Who am I?

I was a yo-yo dieter and binge eater for 30 years. I had lost and regained 25 pounds 5 times over that period. With each loss and regain, my weight would climb even higher. In my 20s, my highest weight was 130. In my 30s, my highest weight was 140. In my 40s, I hit my highest weight of 175 and got down to 130 for a day and then it crept back up to 150. At this point, I became a vegan to improve my health and try to get control of my soaring cholesterol numbers.

It worked somewhat but I was still a binge eater and food addict. I found plenty of foods that were technically vegan. But they were still super fattening and definitely not health promoting.

I became a Registered Holistic Nutritionist. I wanted to help myself and live in congruence with my beliefs. In natural nutrition school we learned health promoting practices for all kinds of problems. I needed to focus on the areas that were affecting me personally. Sustainable and health promoting weight loss.

I used myself as a guinea pig. I tried juice cleanses, raw food diets, and hormone injections. I swallowed enough supplements to make me rattle when I walked. I gained and lost the same 10 pounds for two years. I was still a fat vegan. I didn't look or feel like the example of good health I wanted to present to my clients. I felt like a fraud. But I was determined to solve this problem. I was determined to be that shining beacon of health.

It wasn't until I learned to SUBTRACT things from my diet rather than to ADD them that the weight came off and stayed off. There is no pill or supplement that will magically solve this problem for you.

Now I am congruent with my beliefs and message. I walk the talk every day and I am more than ready to share what I have learned with as many people as possible.

I have finally solved this problem that had plagued me for my entire adult life. I want so desperately for you to succeed as I have and solve this problem for good. I want you to be free from the constant battle in your head about your weight, food and diets. Then you can concentrate on the real reason you were put on earth. I want to free you of the shackles of excess fat. Not only so you will look your best. But so, you can focus on getting on with your own goals and dreams.

What You are Going to Learn

Not only do I want you to lose the extra fat. I want to make sure you keep it off by establishing a whole new healthy lifestyle. I have designed this book to give you the plan that will set you up for success. This is the map to your weight loss journey. At the end of most chapters I have added some tasks to complete before proceeding. You will have a step-by-step approach to starting and then continuing this journey.

You are going to learn what your goal weight should be. What you need to do to lose the weight and what you need to do to maintain it. This book is different. Once we determine your ideal weight, we start with the calories you need to maintain that weight. There will be no big transition from weight loss to maintenance. You will be able to maintain it because it is the way you have been eating from Day 1. Without hunger or deprivation.

In Chapter 1, I cover how to set yourself up for success. You need to know where you are starting from so you can get very clear on your weight and state of health. We will set up a goal book. You can track your progress through the process and help you plan for the upcoming weeks.

In Chapter 2, I explain how to calculate important numbers unique to you. These numbers will help you to truly know if you are on track or not. I also introduce a mind-blowing fact that no one else talks about. It explains why you can never be full on a weigh-and-measure diet.

In Chapter 3, we break down foods into categories. The categories are based on calorie density and nutrient density. By the end of this chapter, it will be clear why it was so difficult for you in the past to lose and then maintain a weight loss. It is a matter of numbers.

Chapter 4 discusses the modern-day food traps of sugar, oil and salt. I cover how they are undermining your health and weight loss objectives. I also offer solutions to the problem. You'll learn how to get great tasting food without these three addictive things.

In Chapter 5, will be when you really start implementing what you have learned so far. The steps that you take in this chapter are critical to your achievement of your weight loss and weight maintenance. They will set you up for success for the coming weeks, months and years. It's all about your environment.

Chapter 6 is the time to get out your knives. I show you how to do a week's worth of bulk cooking so that you will be ready to go. I also break down what to prepare on three days of the bulk cooking. If you can do it in one day, you are a rock star in the kitchen!

In Chapter 7, I teach you about the psychological dangers of being a scale monkey. We look at what you are actually weighing. And what has to happen in your body to lose fat.

Chapter 8 deals with the 'what ifs'. I get real about emotional eating, binge eating, cramming and food triggers. Once you know why you engage in these behaviors, you are forearmed to prevent slip ups. Knowledge is power.

Chapter 9 teaches you how to deal with the haters. In this chapter you learn how to handle people who question your new way of eating. It is non-confrontational and you will be amazed how well it works.

In Chapter 10, I close the circle with some unanswered questions that I didn't address in other parts of the book. Some questions are so off topic, I felt that it would be distracting to include in the other chapters. But I felt that they were definitely important enough to include here. I cover topics like motivation, detoxification, and supplementation. I also talk about other stuff that doesn't end in *-ation*!

Now that you know what you are in for, let's get to it…

Chapter One

Getting Started

Most conventional diets have it wrong when it comes to goal setting. You set an arbitrary goal of X pounds to lose before this or that event. Everyone wants to look their best before a wedding, a class reunion, the summer, or another event. They set either an unattainable goal or a goal that is attainable but won't be sustainable.

That's the pattern of yo-yo dieters. There is always a good reason to start another diet. There is always something coming up in the future that you are determined to look your best for. Why? Why do you want to look your best for that event? Why? Ask yourself this question. Chances are that your answer will be something like. I want people to say how marvelous I look. 'Have you lost weight? You look fantastic!'

You are highly motivated to get this approval from your tribe. You will starve yourself to get this approval. If you don't reach your arbitrary goal, your self esteem is in the toilet. You end up having a lousy time thinking about how people may be judging you.

If you lose weight but people don't say anything, you feel

even more despondent than before. So, what happens at this point. You throw up your hands say what's the use and return to your 'normal' way of eating.

Then up goes your weight, down goes your expectations. You regain the weight because the diet was unsustainable. Then you wait until there is something else to diet for and a new diet is selected and off to the races you go. Does this sound familiar?

There is a much better way of goal setting. Do not wait until some distant day in the future to receive the love and approval and accolades from others. You will still have your internal audience to answer to. It took me years to realize that people are more concerned about how *they* look. How *they* measure up to the tribe. You need to get *your* self esteem from *yourself.* But more on this later.

Visit Your Doctor

First of all, you should get a physical. Get the facts straight about where you are starting from. It may take a week or two to get an appointment for your physical. It's okay to start your journey before the appointment but at least you'll have this scheduled within the first month.

There will be three things you will need to do with your doctor:

1. A blood test for total cholesterol and triglycerides and a blood sugar reading. It is important to know these numbers to see what needs improvement. You also need to get your blood pressure checked. The results of these tests may affect the

dosage of medication you are currently on. That's if you are on any.

2. You will want to weigh in. This weight will be far more accurate than your bathroom scale. In the future, it will give your doctor clear proof of how successful you have been on this new way of eating. And get your height checked. I found out to my dismay that I have shrank in my fifties which was pretty depressing. An accurate height and weight will help you to calculate your BMI (Body Mass Index). We will do this later to help determine a good starting goal weight.

3. Tell your doctor that you are starting a whole-foods plant-based (WFPB) diet. This is to see if it will help improve your health. It is important to discuss this with your doctor. You may have medication that will need adjusting over time.

For example, if you are on a statin medication this will affect your cholesterol level. Or you might be on pills or injections to control your blood sugar. The amount of medication you take for any condition is based on your current weight and state of health. Your doctor will want to closely watch your progress. He may need to adjust your medications as you lose weight and your general health and diet improves.

If your doctor does not support your decision to try a WFPB diet get another opinion. Naturopath doctors are more supportive of you improving your lifestyle rather than prescribing medication.

No one gets rid of heart disease by taking a statin and no one is cured of diabetes by taking metformin. It is time to work in partnership with your doctor to make lifestyle changes for the better.

If your doctor has questions. You can tell him that this diet is based on various whole food plant-based programs. The following doctors have similar programs: Dr. Caldwell Esselstyn, Dr. Dean Ornish, Dr. John McDougall, and Dr. Alan Goldhamer. Once you have had the doctor's visit and blood work, you are ready to start the program. The doctor will have those results on file for you to get at a later date.

Your lab work and tests from your physical give us a before picture of your health. This information helps you and your doctor see your progress to good health. Your journey may take 6 months to a year to reach your ideal weight. Or, in the case of those who need to lose a significant amount of weight, 2 or 3 years down the road. But the journey is well worth it when you have excellent health, fitness and self confidence at the end of it.

How to Choose a healthy goal weight based on your Body Mass Index (BMI)

Basing it on your high school grad weight or your friend's weight is not scientific. Determining your body mass index (BMI) is a good guide for most people. The exception is body builders. They have more muscle mass than the average person. As muscle weighs more than fat, the BMI is inaccurate. Based on their height and weight they would come out as having an obese BMI. But, if you are reading this book, I am betting that you do not fall into this category so let's press on.

The BMI is a good guide to determine a healthy goal weight. It is also what your doctor uses to determine your classification and risk factors. There are lots of BMI calculators on the internet that you can use. They need information such as your age, sex, height and weight. For the purposes of this book, I will be using the example of the average North American woman. The average woman is 5 feet 4 inches tall. She is 40 years old. And sadly, she weighs 170 pounds. When we plug these numbers into the BMI calculator it shows she has a BMI of 29.2. That's in the high end of the overweight category. (Go to the TASKS at the end of this chapter and I have added some sites that will calculate your BMI.)

Her healthy BMI range would be 108 to 145 pounds. Notice that this is almost a 50-pound range. How do we determine the correct range for our average woman based on this range? We measure her wrist.

To determine a better range, we need to take into consideration the size of her frame. Is she big boned? Slight? Average? You can determine this my measuring your wrist. Rather than putting in a chart, you can find your frame size on the internet. (Again, go to the TASKS at the end of this chapter.)

As with everything else about our average example woman, her frame is also average. So, we have determined that her BMI range is 108 – 145 pounds. Her first goal weight will be 145 pounds. That means an initial loss of 35 pounds is required to get her out of the overweight range. That is an awesome starting point for a goal.

Once you have determined your BMI range you will use the top range of your BMI for your first goal weight. By the time you reach the top end of your BMI, you will look great, be healthy and have much better self esteem. You won't want to go back to your old way of eating. By continuing to eat this way, your body will naturally find the right weight for you within this range.

If you have a medium frame like our average woman, your ultimate goal weight will be somewhere in the middle of the range. For her that is 120 - 132 pounds. Not so light that she looks like a cadaver and family is threatening an intervention. But not so heavy that friends and family are saying it is such a shame that she ballooned up again.

If you eat this way and make it your new lifestyle, you will not want to go back. You will no longer feel lethargic and sick with aches and pains. You will no longer worry if you are going to have a heart attack or stroke. You will know for certainty that you are doing everything you can to protect your good health. You are ensuring that you have an excellent quality of life to the end of your years.

The Goal Book

Your goal book doesn't need to be anything fancy. I buy mine at the dollar store. You can get a 250-page spiral notebook at the dollar store which is good for at least 6 months to get you started. I also do my book in pencil. So, while you are at the store, buy pencils, a sharpener, an eraser and a ruler if you don't already have them. You also need a measuring tape for your measurements.

There are 4 pages you will be starting off making in your book. The first two you will complete only once for the entire book. The last two you will be putting in weekly to prepare for the upcoming week.

Love Letter

On the first page of your goal book write a letter to yourself. Set goals by writing a letter to yourself dated 1 year from today. In the letter write about your successes with your health and weight goals. Say how proud you are of yourself. Go into as much detail as you wish to really get yourself excited about the process.

Weight and Measurement Chart

On the back of the first page, you will draw a weight and measurement chart. You can find an example of this in Appendix 1. The example has a January start but it's an example. You don't have to wait until the beginning of the year or even the beginning of the month to start. Adjust the chart to your own start date and then you will weigh and measure on that date the following month and so on.

Once you have drawn your chart it's time to weigh and measure yourself. Weigh yourself and write it in the chart. Then measure your bust/chest, waist (the narrowest part), abdomen (so the tape is at belly button level), and hips. These are the four measurements. The abdomen measurement is an important and somewhat depressing measurement at first. It can be a visual indicator of heart concerns. Let's get the bad news upfront. Now that we are taking action, those numbers will get smaller every month.

Now comes the fun part. Notice that your chart has REAL and GOAL spaces. Fill in your starting weight and measurements in the month you are starting in the REAL spaces. (see the example if you get confused.)

On this program you can lose 2 pounds of fat every month. If you have over 100 pounds to lose you may lose as much as 5 pounds per month. Under the goal space for each month in the weight boxes, write down your goal weight for each month.

You will lose about 1/2 an inch from each measurement per month. Under the measurement boxes, write down your goal measurements for each month. So, every month each measurement goes down ½ an inch. (Again, see appendix 1 if this is confusing.)

APPENDIX 1: SAMPLE WEIGH AND MEASURE CHART

DATE	JAN	FEB	MAR	APR	MAY	JUN
GOAL WEIGHT		*148*	*146*	*144*	*142*	*140*
REAL	**150**					
GOAL CHEST/BUST		*39.5*	*39*	*38.5*	*38*	*37.5*
REAL	**40**					
GOAL WAIST						
REAL						
GOAL ABDOMEN						
REAL						
GOAL HIPS						
REAL						

Note: Obviously, you can start your journey in any month on any day. Just change the months on the top.

The numbers in *italics* are an example of how you will start. Fill in your starting weight and measurements and then write in: a 2 lb loss per month and a ½ inch loss per month on each measurement in the goal section for each measurement. You can print off the 12-month Weigh and Measure Chart template on my website: www.karenwarwickrhn.com.

Now we have some realistic goals. Look at your new weight and measurements in month 12! You'll be at least 24 pounds lighter. You'll have taken off at least 6 inches off of each measurement. Absolutely fantastic! Imagine how great you will feel in your new body. You may not have reached your ultimate goal but it's definitely a big step in the right direction.

You will find that at the end of the first month you will probably lose more than two pounds. But remember this could be water retention. Do not adjust your goal numbers yet. Three months from now you may hit a plateau and not be losing as your body is adjusting. This gives you a cushion for the month if you don't lose anything. When this notebook is full and you need to start another, this will be the time to make adjustments on your new chart. I found that I lost about 5 pounds a month at first then it varied. But one thing is more consistent. It's that ½ inch off of your measurements every month. That's the real goal because no one sees the scale number but you.

Weekly Target Activities Chart

The second chart is your Weekly Target Activities Chart. (See appendix 2). You will put this on the front of the second page of your notebook. This chart is a great tool and highly motivating to get you hitting your daily targets. You are not aiming for perfection but shoot for 80% of your targets every day. You will be making this target chart every week for the upcoming weeks.

In the example Appendix 2, some writing is in **bold**. This is necessary information to include in your chart. These are the targets that you will need to check off every day to be successful on this plan. The writing in *italics* are examples of things *I* need to do every day to make me feel good about myself. Feel free to add anything in here that you know you should be doing to feel good about yourself. Make it fun and easily attainable.

APPENDIX 2: TARGET ACTIVITIES CHART (EXAMPLE)

	M	T	W	TH	F	S	S
LAST NIGHT'S SLEEP	*8*	*7*	*6.5*	*8*			
BREAKFAST VEGGIES	*X*	*X*	*X*	*X*			
2ND BREAKFAST STARCH	*X*		*X*	*X*			
FRUIT	*X*	*X*	*X*	*X*			
LUNCH STARCH	*X*	*X*	*X*	*X*			
DINNER STARCH	*X*	*X*		*X*			
WALK DOG							
SHOWER							
JOURNAL							
YOGA							
BRUSH TEETH/ TAKE PILLS							

Note: The bold text **is required in your table** for this plan. The *italics* text are examples of what I do every day. This target activities chart is based on Dr. Doug Lisle's chart on his website:

https://esteemdynamics.com/. His version is in the member's section. If you become a member, you can use his version. Or copy out my framework here into your Goal Book.

Daily Sheets

Starting with the back of the Weekly Target Activities Chart and the next three pages you will be writing out your Daily Sheet for the week. This includes your meal plan for the day, appointments and food/mood journal. (See appendix 3). For now, you will be putting in the framework which is the writing in **bold** in the example. Allow 2 spaces between each meal on your page. This will leave you lots of space for your notes.

APPENDIX 3: DAILY SHEET (EXAMPLE)

MONDAY (DAY OF WEEK)   *JUNE 10* (DATE)
B: *BIG SALAD WITH TABBOULEH*
B2: *APPLE CRUMBLE. FRESH FRUIT*
L: *BAKED POTATO, CHEEZY SAUCE, BRUSSELS SPROUTS*
D: *CHILI ON RICE, VEGGIES AND HUMMUS*
APPOINTMENTS: *CHIROPRACTOR 10:40*
NOTES: *This is where I write about my day. I usually do this the next morning. I reflect back on my mood for the day, my challenges and successes. Even mundane things that are not food related are written here. These notes are important because in a few months time you may want to look back at things that may be triggers for you.*

Journaling

Okay let's go on to journaling. In your goal book for every day, you will have a few lines where you can write notes about your day. Ask yourself some questions. How you are feeling? What victories you had? What challenges did you face? How are you feeling about the process? Stuff you have to do. Whatever you want to write. All you need are 3 sentences not a novel. Do it at the end of the day or the next morning and reflect back on the previous day. This doesn't seem like much but over a long period, you will gain some great insights

When your journey is done, you might want to write a book or talk about your success story. You will have all the details in your journal. It is also important to remember where you came from and how you felt at the beginning of your journey. Then you can really appreciate how far you have come. You have turned your life, your self confidence, and your health around.

Describe how you are feeling physically and emotionally. Everyone will have good days and bad days. Notice when you are tired, sleepy, overloaded at work or stressed out. That's part of being alive. Make note of these feelings as well. It will help you when you want to reflect back on things.

Work the Plan Every Day

The Target Sheet is based on the findings of Dr. Lisle who is a brilliant evolutionary psychologist. This is what I used and it really works.

So, here's the plan. You follow a superior plant-based diet every day and you check off the boxes on your Target Sheet. You don't have to be perfect. You are managing a problem just like an addict does and this is a daily practice. Every day, your internal audience will give you a rating of how well you did this day. So, aim for at least 80% of your daily targets every day.

As days go by, your internal audience will respect your dedication and diligence. Every day that you have hit 80% of your targets your internal audience will be giving you a gold star. Your self esteem will go up and as a result your self confidence will also increase. You will start to feel good about yourself. You will be meeting those targets every day because it feels good to do so.

You won't be perfect. But you will be good enough for an A. Some days you will be perfect. Some days not so much. But the result is a healthy self esteem and glowing self confidence that comes with doing an A level job every day.

You will not need that approval from outside sources. You know in your heart that you are doing your very best you can every day. And sure, you have more to go but you are working on the problem. You are becoming a good life manager for the most important person in your life, YOU!

By consistently hitting your targets, your weight will stabilize to your ideal weight. The length of your journey is not important. It is the journey itself that is important to your health and your self esteem.

Your monthly weight and measurement chart will be proof of your progress. When you look over your goal numbers at the end of the year you can see how much better your numbers will be. Then the following year, if you have more to lose, they will only get better.

If you have reached your goal within the year, you can still continue with the measurement chart. On the chart either keep the numbers the same for each month, or tweak them depending on how satisfied you are.

For example, I have always been blessed with nice boobs. But as I got heavier and heavier, they of course got bigger and bigger. As I lost weight, they got smaller. When I got down to my ideal weight, I didn't want to become so thin that my boobs were gone. All I would be left with would be two empty skin sacks. So, I decided that 35 inches was my goal measurement for that particular body part. You see what I'm saying? I know what my ideal weight needs to be to keep my boobs.

So now that you have set up the basics to succeed. In the next chapter I talk about two exciting and seldom talked about facts about sustainable weight loss. One fact will be specific. Just for you. The other will teach you how to lose weight but never go hungry.

TASKS:

1. Visit your doctor. Get height, weight and blood pressure checked. Get blood work for cholesterol, triglycerides and blood sugar. Tell your doctor about your plan to start a whole foods plant-based diet.
2. Calculate your BMI. You can use this website: Adult BMI Calculator | Healthy Weight, Nutrition, and Physical Activity | CDC or BMI Calculator.
3. Measure your wrist to determine your frame size: Body Frame Size Chart - Fitness Vigil, or Calculating body frame size: MedlinePlus Medical Encyclopedia Image.

4. Determine your ultimate goal range by subtracting the low number from the high number in the BMI range and divide it by 3. This gives you the number of pounds for each frame. For example, our average woman's BMI range is 108 – 145 pounds.
   145 – 108 = 37 pounds divided by 3 = 12 pounds.
   So, a small frame would have a range of 108 -120 pounds, a medium frame 120 -132 pounds, a large frame 132 - 145 pounds.

5. Buy yourself a small (6-inch x 9-inch) 250 page or 500-page notebook from the dollar store. You will need pencils, erasers, pencil sharpener, and a ruler. You need a cloth measuring tape and maybe some kid's stickers. **

6. Your goal book will contain your letter to yourself, the monthly measurement sheet. A weekly target sheet and then 4 pages back-to-back to do the upcoming 7 days for meal plans and daily journal entries. Before you start your will want to make your framework for the pages based on the examples I have provided. You can write your love letter, make your weight and measurement chart framework, write your daily target sheet, and your daily meal plan and journal entry sheets for the week. This is just the framework at this point. The specifics of menu planning are covered in Chapter 5. So, you can set aside your goal book for now until you have read through Chapter 5.

** Chef AJ uses this method. I still do this every day because it makes me strangely happy. Give yourself a gold star or some other kids sticker on every calendar day that you are

100% abstinent from SOFAS (Sugar, oil, flour, alcohol, salt). Soon you will have days then months behind you of colorful stickers blocking up the calendar. It is a great visual of your daily success. Even though it might seem silly, you will be surprised how proud you will become of those stickers.

Chapter Two

How Many Calories and How Much Food?

It is true that you can lose weight on a calorie restrictive diet. I know that I have in the past. The problem with a calorie restrictive diet is simply this. The number of calories they allow you will not be specific to your unique body. Say that for your height and weight you need 1500 calories per day to survive. Now, you can weigh and measure your tiny portions of food and eat your 1500 per day. But it really isn't a lot of food and some of it certainly isn't nutritious. You will get hungry and that is the problem. Maybe you can tough it out for a month, 2 months or even 3. But eventually you are going to crack. Your body requires nutrients and satiety. It's a biological fact.

You can only hold your breath for so long until you will need to breath. You can only go so long without sleep until your body will force you to sleep. You can only go without water for so long as well. The same is true for food. Your body is a survival mechanism. It will do anything to survive and at some point, it will override all that willpower and force you to eat to satiety.

Calculating your Daily Calorie Requirements

Okay, my BMI (Body Mass Index) range was 89-119 pounds. My top range number was 119. This would be my first goal weight. 119. That meant I had 26 pounds to lose at 145. That's a lot of weight on such a short woman.

Next, I found a calorie calculator online. This is to determine how many calories I needed to lose and maintain a weight of 119. You put in your age, sex, height, and **goal weight**. Then you take two readings. (Go to the TASKS at the end of this chapter for links to BMR calculators.)

1. Calculate you BMR (Basal Metabolism Rate). This is the number which calculates how many calories it takes to keep you alive and healthy. It's enough calories to keep your heart beating, and your organs functioning. My BMR is 1005 calories per day.

2. Then there is a chart for exercise level. I chose that my activity level was 1-3 times per week which is not true. But might as well get the low range for those days of binge-watching TV. This was 1381 calories per day.

So now I had my range. 1005-1381 calories per day. This way I know for certain how many calories per day are right for me. I know that going below 1005 is dangerous to my health. And I know that going over 1381 without activity I will stall my weight loss and I may not reach my goal weight.

Let's do our calculations of our average North American woman. Remember she is 5' 4'', 170 pounds and 40 years old. Her healthy BMI is 108 to 145 pounds. So, we will put in 145 pounds into the calculator. Her BMR is 1513 calories per day.

I have set her exercise level at 1-3 times per week. This is 1805 calories per day. Now we have her range. 1513 – 1805. She needs 1513 calories per day to keep her healthy and under 1805 per day without much activity to lose weight and then maintain her weight at 145 pounds. We also know that our average woman has been eating significantly over 1805 calories per day for some time since she currently weighs 170 pounds.

You see, this is the problem with generalization. This is the problem with standardized diets. They don't take into account the specifics of your individual qualities. I tell you I had happily gone along with *the average* calorie intake for women. That's 2000 calories to maintain weight and 1500 calories to lose weight. You can see now that when you do the math. If I ate 2000 calories per day to maintain my weight, I would be overconsuming 619 calories each and every day. No wonder I couldn't maintain it. Our average woman would be overconsuming 195 calories per day. The weight gain would have been slower than mine but she would get there eventually.

With my low range of 1005 – 1381 calories I had a problem. How could I possibly eat to satisfaction on so few calories per day? I was sure that one plant-based burger with fries and onion rings would use up my entire calorie allotment. I again cursed the fact that I was so darn short (and apparently shrinking) not for the first time in my life.

I had to find a way to get in enough satisfying food every day but stay within my calorie range. I did not want to go back to calorie counting. What a life sucking preoccupation with food that can be. I had spent most of my life thinking about food. How many calories, can I get away with? What can I eat now and be satisfied? I was determined to find another way. And that's when I finally learned about and embraced calorie density.

4 Pounds of Food

Did you know that women eat an average of 4 pounds of food every day? Four pounds on average is enough to please your hunger drive. Men eat an average of 5 pounds. There are exceptions ranging from 3 to 7 pounds per day. But the average each day of the year is 4 pounds of food.

Now this can come from any kind of food. Considering this, I had a big dilemma. How could I get 4 pounds of food per day and still get under my 1381 calories per day? Here are some extreme examples of what 4 pounds of food could look like:

- 4 pounds of raw non-starchy vegetables will provide 400 calories
- 4 pounds of fruit will provide approximately 1200 calories
- 4 pounds of starches (starchy vegetables, whole grains, legumes). They provide a range of 1600 - 2400 calories

Now these are reasonable…. I could work with these. But then let's look at the foods that keep your fat or increase your weight:

- 4 pounds of avocados will provide 3000 calories.
- 4 pounds of refined complex carbohydrates and dairy (e.g., baked goods, sugar, ice cream, cheese). They will provide a range between 4800 – 7200 calories.
- 4 pounds of chocolate will provide 10,000 calories.
- 4 pounds of nuts, seeds, and nut butters will provide

11,200 calories.

- 4 pounds of all fats and oils will provide 16,000 calories.

Now look at these numbers as if these were dollars that we were spending rather than calories. You can see how expensive eating a calorie rich diet would be.

For example, I've only got 1381 measly calories to buy with, there are some foods that are simply too darned expensive.

So how can I get my 4 pounds of food per day and stay within my range. Well let's get the fewest calories in first. The ones with the lowest calorie density but the highest nutrient density and work our way up from there.

- 2 pounds of vegetables provides 200 calories
- 1 pound of fruit provides 300 calories
- 1 pound of starchy vegetables, grains and legumes average 500 calories

So that is 1000 calories for 4 pounds of food. I can still eat almost 4 extra pounds of vegetables or 1 pound of fruit or close to a pound of starches to reach my 1381 calories per day. And you can probably eat even more. That is impressive! You certainly won't go hungry eating this way. To ensure that I concentrate on the low-calorie food first, I sequence my meals this way.

1. Raw salad
2. Steamed or roasted non-starchy vegetables
3. Starches

This way you get a lot of low-calorie nutrition in first followed by a satiating starch. You keep your calories low yet you are comfortably full and satisfied by the end of the meal.

You can eat your fresh fruit any time during the day when you feel a little hungry or as a dessert.

The best part is you have already determined your calorie range at your goal weight. Not at your current starting weight. This means that you will have learned how to eat to maintain your goal weight or even lower from Day 1. There will be no transition from 'a diet' to a 'maintenance plan'. You will know from Day 1 what you need to eat to lose the weight and maintain it for the rest of your life.

In the next chapter, you will learn which foods to choose so that you won't feel hungry and yet still lose the extra weight.

TASKS

1. Calculate your BMR (Basal Metabolism Rate) using a calorie calculator. You can go to <u>BMR Calculator</u> or <u>BMR Calculator - Calculate your BMR and Calorie Needs</u>. Determine your activity level in order to have your range of calories you can consume in a day.

2. Really let the concept of 4 pounds of food sink in (or 5 for men). You can see how your old way of eating was guaranteeing that you would steadily gain weight. You can also see why weigh-and-measure diets would always keep you feeling hungry. You would not be able to get your 4 or 5 pounds of food in while 'spending your calories' on high calorie foods. We need to take into account calorie density.

Chapter Three

Calorie Density versus Nutrient Density

First of all, I want to say that this is not my idea. As a matter of fact, I am following in the footsteps of many great doctors and specialists. It is the only thing that has allowed me to reach and maintain my ideal weight. I want to continue to spread this important message. The message is that it is easy to lose and maintain your weight if you eat the right foods. This is the only thing you have to worry about.

So how can we keep our bodies happy and still lose weight. Well, the trick is to eat what your body was originally designed to eat. The superior plant-based diet has all the nutrients your body needs to restore health. There is enough water and fiber to feel satiated. And you will lose the excess weight until your body is at its ideal weight. And you will stay there as long as you continue to eat the right foods.

LOW CALORIE DENSITY AND HIGH NUTRIENT DENSITY

These are the foods that you want to focus on. Eating them you will get your healthy four pounds of food and still lose weight. These foods are whole foods. They are found in nature and contain vitamins, minerals, antioxidants, phytochemicals and micronutrients. They also contain fiber and water which creates bulk and increases satiety. To get the most nutrition try to eat as many organic, locally grown foods as you can. Also eat vegetables and fruit that are in season. This helps to keep the costs down. All four food groups have two things in common. They are fiber and water. The two things that the body needs to lose weight and maintain it in a healthy way.

Non-Starchy Vegetables – 100 calories per pound

These foods will make up a great deal of your diet and the variety is amazing. You can eat as much as you can of these foods without having to control portion sizes or weighing and measuring. They average less than 100 calories a pound. This includes all the non-starchy vegetables. Peppers, carrots, radishes, onions, garlic, tomatoes and anything green. I can go on and on.

At only 100 calories a pound that is a lot of vegetables. They are loaded with fiber and water which create bulk and increase satiety. They are living foods just like you are a living animal. Living foods are what your cells need.

At only 100 calories a pound you can eat as many of them as you wish. Ideally, you will start each meal with these vegetables. This is to slow down your eating time. Studies show that people who take longer than 18 minutes to eat their meal do not have problems with weight. It takes this long to signal the brain that you have eaten.

Raw vegetables need a lot of chewing so they naturally

slow down your speed of eating. This makes it easy for you to make a meal last 18 minutes. They are also loaded with fiber and water so they fill you up. They activate the stretch receptors in your stomach. This signals the brain that you have eaten. So, start every meal with a salad or steamed vegetables and/or a bowl of vegetable soup. And save your starches until the end of the meal.

Again, I could go through great lists of vegetables with all their health benefits which is a book in itself. I am simply going to mention one category, leafy greens. These are the most important for weight loss.

Eating leafy greens is one of the best ways to prevent disease and promote health. They are full of fiber and low in calories, which make them a perfect food to support your weight-loss goals.

Leafy green vegetables contain structures called thylakoids. Thylakoids can help to reduce feelings of hunger. Eating thylakoids affects hormones that modulate hunger and satiety. These hormones are related to your appetite and the desire to eat.

Also, thylakoids help prevent a drop in blood sugar after meals. With stable blood sugar, you won't get cravings. All green vegetables contain thylakoids. But leafy vegetables are some of the richest sources. Some of the top leafy green benefits include:

1. Blood pressure - There are high levels of calcium and potassium in nearly *all* leafy greens. This is beneficial for lowering blood pressure.

2. Type 2 diabetes - Leafy greens reduce the risk of type 2 diabetes. Greens are high in fibre and water. So, they slow the absorption of carbohydrates into your bloodstream after meals. And the fiber found in leafy greens helps you stabilize blood sugar.

3. Heart Disease - There is a high folate concentration in leafy greens. This can reduce your risk of cardiovascular disease. Leafy greens can also help lower cholesterol levels.

4. Inflammation - Leafy greens are rich in antioxidants like flavonoids and carotenoids. These are crucial in reducing inflammation. Greens are also alkaline which helps neutralize the acids in your body.

Green leafy vegetables help to reduce your appetite. They help you lose weight, and reduce your risk for disease. That's why it's always a good idea to have salad for breakfast and set yourself up for a day of success.

Fruit – 300 calories per pound

Fresh fruit is under 300 calories a pound. Beautiful fresh fruit no matter which kind will add the sweetness to your diet that is oh so satisfying.

I remember when I was a child. My tastebuds had not been corrupted by hyper-palatable overprocessed sugary foods. I remember what it was like to pick and eat fresh raspberries and strawberries that were warmed by the sun. Apples and pears from the tree in the fall. The neighbor who had a peach tree in his yard and gave me a nice warm peach over the fence. Absolutely fantastic.

Fruit is also loaded with fiber and water so dig into some of your favorites. It's great to have free reign to eat a pound of delicious fruit a day and still lose the weight. Also, you can experiment with some new fruits that you have never tried.

I tried a pomelo one day because it was on sale at my supermarket and I've never looked back. They are fantastic. It's a like a giant grapefruit but sweeter and not as tangy. It is a lot of work to peel and get into but well worth the effort.

Fresh fruit has lots of nutrition that everyone seems to know about but doesn't seem to eat. The citrus family has loads of vitamin C which is a water-soluble vitamin so it needs to be replenished every day. Eating this way, you are strengthening your immunity with delicious citrus fruits.

Starchy Vegetables, Whole Grains and Legumes – 400 – 600 calories per pound

The next category is unrefined complex carbohydrates. They are approximately 400 to 600 calories per pound. You may ask what is an unrefined complex carbohydrate. Well, it is a food that you can recognize as being in its natural state. This group triggers the satiety pleasing mechanism in your body.

Starchy Vegetables

This includes starchy vegetables like potatoes, sweet potatoes, peas, corn and the squash family. You may ask 'how much is a pound of potatoes? I thought they were fattening.' It's not true. It's what you put on them that makes them fattening. One pound of potatoes equals 3 ¼ cups for 354 calories. That's a lot of potato in one pound.

Grains

All the delicious whole grains are also included. Grains like rice, quinoa, oats, and millet. I have not included wheat as no one eats wheat in its natural form anymore. It is processed in the form of flour. It is then baked into a concoction much higher than 600 calories a pound.

Here's some mind-blowing news. Calories do NOT change when you cook food in just water. There are 503 calories in a pound of brown rice. One-pound equals 2 ½ cups raw rice. When cooked that 2 ½ cups raw turns into 9 cups cooked. I don't know about you but I couldn't possibly eat 9 cups of rice. So, there's no need to measure your rice servings. Just eat as much as you please. All those slim Asians can't be wrong. Again, it is what you put on your rice that adds the calories so stick to plain rice and you can't go wrong.

Legumes

Then we have the legume family which includes all the beans and lentils. Fantastic for nutrition and satiety.

Beans are an inexpensive staple in a plant-based diet. In their dry form they keep forever. Perfect for emergencies or in preparation for the zombie apocalypse. They are loaded with fiber and B-vitamins along with many other vitamins and minerals. Here's a list of the benefits of legumes:

- Beans are an excellent source of protein, and complemented with grains or vegetables are a complete source of protein.
- Legumes contain protective fiber which helps eliminate

toxins from the body. Recent research indicates that they contain several anti-cancer agents.

- All legumes contain a good source of essential fatty acids - omega 3 and 6.
- Legumes are known to lower cholesterol levels significantly, control insulin and blood sugar, and lower blood pressure.

HIGH CALORIE DENSITY AND HIGH NUTRIENT DENSITY

If you need to gain weight, eating these foods is the healthiest way. After a long hospital recovery, my husband who has always been slim came out of there scary thin. I got his weight back up by letting him indulge in these healthy but calorie dense foods.

But, if you want to lose weight, these foods are off limits at least until you reach your ideal weight. Then you can reintroduce small quantities of them. But be very careful. They are super dense in calories and are so delicious they are very easy to overeat.

If one of these is a food trigger for you. I mean you just can't stop eating them once you start. Or it triggers you to eat processed foods like guacamole with tortilla chips. You should avoid them entirely. They will not help to keep your weight stable at your ideal weight. They could trigger a binge. But, they are loaded with nutrition so they are worthy of noting.

Avocados – 750 calories per pound

Avocados are 750 calories a pound and are fantastic as a spread, or in a smoothie or, of course, in guacamole. A serving size of avocado is actually 1/5th of an avocado. Only a 5th! That's nothing.

My Scottish blood rises when I think about eating only 1/5th of an avocado over 5 consecutive days. Every day you have to rewrap the avocado and put it back in the fridge for tomorrow. It will look browner and more gross than it did the day before. It's sad. If you are going to partake in avocado when you are at your goal weight, save it for a party. Everyone will get a serving size and there won't be any left overs calling your name in the middle of the night.

Raw Nuts and Seeds – 2800 calories per pound

My favorite category is high in nutrient density and super high in calories. That is raw nuts, seeds, nut butters and tahini. These delicious foods kept my last 20 pounds on me for over 2 years. I could not lose weight and incorporate these healthy fats. This kept me happy. But it also kept me a fat vegan.

These foods are 2,800 calories a pound. Some doctors promoting the plant-based lifestyle use a lot of nuts and seeds in their recipes. And believe me I enjoyed each one of them. But these people may not have had weight problems. They have never started out from behind the eight ball with 20 or more pounds to lose.

I finally discovered Chef AJ. She had also been a fat vegan. Through her teachings, I realized how I was sabotaging all my diligent efforts. I was incorporating lots of nut, seed, and avocado-based dressings and sauces into my daily diet. I knew they were healthy. But nuts, seeds and avocado aren't necessary for the body to function optimally. Especially when you have lots of fat to lose. I had forgotten about, or was in denial about, the calories.

Once I cut out these foods the weight just fell off my body. And as I am against the whole weigh and measure philosophy, I have rarely added them back. If the recipe will be greatly enhanced by them and I feel that I can keep it more as a once-in-awhile treat, I will add a few nuts or seeds.

You may ask, what about your healthy fats, don't you need fat in your diet. If fat is a trigger for you and you have enough fat on your ass, you will be just fine without adding more fat to your diet. You can still get in some healthy fats but you need to control the amount. I add 1 tablespoon or chia, hemp or ground flax to my dressings and sauces which I make in bulk. So, I can control the amount of fat intake and yet get the good fats into my body. Also remember that all plants contain a little fat. You'll be just fine without it.

HIGH CALORIE DENSITY AND LOW NUTRIENT DENSITY

Highly Processed Foods – 1,200 - 1,800 calories per pound

Now we get into the dead foods. There is nothing nutritionally redeemable about them. What limited good news there is about these foods is all bullshit. It is propaganda set out by the manufacturers and producers to give you a glimmer of hope. The truth is hard to take but here it is. These foods keep you fat and sickly. And they go a long way in ensuring that you will stay that way. Until the day your body finally gives up treading water and you die.

These foods are processed foods not found in nature. They contain few if any micronutrients and little to no fiber or water. They also contribute little to satiety that's why it is so easy to eat a lot of them. They have also been engineered to be highly addictive. They contain the combination of sugar, fat and salt. They also contain flavor enhancers and MSG that are engineered to make you keep eating. This category is comprised of refined complex carbohydrates and dairy. They range in calories from 1,200 to 1,800 per pound.

Ice Cream – 1,200 calories per pound

Ice cream is a deadly combination of milk/cream and sugar. The protein in dairy is called casein. According to Dr. Colin Campbell's book *The China Study*, cancer cells in the body can be turned on and off by fiddling with the percentage of casein. Add sugar to the mix which is a fuel for cancer cells you have a deadly combination. So obviously ice cream should never be part of a healthy diet for any reason.

Frozen bananas can be used as a great replacement. Blended frozen bananas or other frozen fruit are called nice cream. It tastes just as decadent and delicious. It has a lot fewer calories and none of the health dangers associated with ice cream.

Bread – 1,400 calories per pound

Next up at 1400 calories per pound is bread. There is nothing like fresh baked bread. It is delicious. But gluten is one of the most common food sensitivities in our diet. Gluten can wreak havoc on the digestive tract by creating little fissures.

These fissures cause something called leaky gut. That's when broken down particles of food leak out of the digestive tract into the blood stream. This causes all kinds of damage.

If you claim that you are not sensitive to gluten, that is possible but realize this. In North America, the amount of gluten that you are consuming in bread today is not the same amount as your grandparents ate. The wheat is a hybrid of what our ancestors ate. It is a shorter plant with a faster growth time. This is so producers can get more growing seasons and more product in a year. Unfortunately, this shorter wheat has much more gluten in it. Wheat is no longer grown to be part of a healthy diet. It is grown to make as much money as possible despite the consequences to our health.

If that doesn't give you pause, think about 1,400 calories per pound. And that's just the bread. I don't know about you but very few people are eating just plain old bread. It is a device used to get more stuff to your mouth without needing a knife and fork. Whether it is a spread. Like avocado, vegan mayo or a nut butter. You can be looking at a diet gone off the rails as soon as you let it pass your lips. Bread has an amazing taste just like all the other foods in this category and that means it tastes like more.

So, what can you use instead of bread? Well either you shrug and don't bother pretending. Or you use things like collard greens for wraps or Romaine lettuce for boats. Both works well but I'm too lazy to bother. A big baked potato stuffed with chili and salsa is super satisfying and delicious. And I guarantee you can only eat one.

Cheese – 1,600 calories per pound

Oh cheese. Cheese is 1,600 calories a pound. And it doesn't take much to make up a pound of cheese. Again, you have the problem with the casein turning your cancer cells on and off. But the bigger problem for weight loss is that the fat content in this is huge.

People seldom eat cheese on its own. It could be because it is so darned dry. Maybe that's why people have it with wine. People like to use cheese to add flavor to things that are already processed and high in calories. Like pastas covered in cheese. If you ate a pound of cheese would that fill up your stomach? Not even close so you would soon be hungry.

What if you took those same calories and ate a compliant food? That would be 3 pounds of potatoes or 16 pounds of carrots do you think you would be full? Yes, you would. Forget the cheese because it can't do anything good for you. It is processed and is super calorie dense. For that cheesy flavor, use nutritional yeast to sprinkle on foods. Or use it in dressings and sauces. You won't be missing a thing.

Sugar – 1,800 calories per pound

Sugar is addictive. It comes in at 1,800 calories a pound. It is a super destructive force in the body. It destroys your teeth but that's what we can see on the outside. It causes inflammation of tissues and joints. It is an essential ingredient in developing Type 2 diabetes. It is acidic in the blood. This causes bone loss as your body tries to balance your blood pH. Your body needs to rob calcium from your bones to reach pH equilibrium.

People who eat a lot of sugar not only have weight problems. They have a difficult addiction to overcome. They also have a food that will contribute to a debilitating disease. Sugar is a legal chemical that destroys lives. Almost as much as any illegal chemical and it is in ubiquitous. It is in everything from ketchup to confectionary.

Sugar is a classic go-to food for anyone who has a binge eating disorder. And you can never get enough of it. Never. It lights up the dopamine releasing circuits in your brain and life is good for a few minutes.

I had a huge problem with sugar when I would binge eat. I would actually add about a cup of brown sugar to a big bowl of ice cream and eat it. Both the ice cream and the brown sugar I bought for my husband. But when I would seriously lose control, there would be no stopping me. If you want to regain your health, keep all sugar out of the house. Use beautiful fresh fruit as a natural sweetener in foods or alone as your dessert.

Chocolate – 2,500 calories per pound

Coming in at a whopping 2,500 calories a pound is chocolate. Wow I am not surprised that it is so addictive. The right blend of cacao and sugar and milk is fantastic. They say that eating chocolate is the same feeling as being in love and that is true. It exquisitely hits on all the dopamine centers in the brain giving you that sweet bliss point. But the difference is that falling in love doesn't give you a fat ass. You say but isn't chocolate good for you? Yes, raw cacao is a great antioxidant but is still high in calories and that's not how you are eating it, is it?

Nothing will make you go off the rails like chocolate. It calls your name in the middle of the night and the chocolate producers know what they are doing. They've got special chocolate treats for every holiday they can muster up an excuse for. Check you calendar. Valentine's day with the heart shaped boxes. Followed by Easter with all kinds of creatures shaped in solid milk chocolate. Then we get a break until Mother's and Father's days. That's when kids run out of ideas or can't spend a lot of money…. here comes more chocolate. Then we get a bit of a reprieve until Halloween. This leads up to more chocolate for the holiday season. Now add in hot chocolate and the year is done. This one 'food' has made me blow my New Year's resolution to lose weight.

Oh…how I have suffered with chocolate as my nemesis. One bite will knock me off track for weeks.

Years ago, when I was in the early days of dating my second husband. I was doing the grocery shopping and the solid Easter bunnies were out. I particularly liked the ones with the Rice Krispies inside. I bought three of them. One for me, one for my boyfriend and one for his daughter. I thought it would be a nice surprise for them on Easter morning to have a chocolate bunny.

I managed to get out of the store parking lot without opening mine but as soon as I got home, I made short work of it. Then it tasted like more. My boyfriend doesn't need a chocolate bunny. He doesn't expect one. So, then I ate his bunny. I stopped there and went on with my day. That night, the house was very quiet except for an almost indiscernible sound like a whisper. It was that third bunny! I was comforted in the thought that no one knew that I had even bought them. Besides the girl didn't seem to like me very much anyway. The shame that followed still haunts me today. And that was just Easter.

Halloween is even worse. I buy those big boxes that contain 120 mini chocolate bars. I buy at least 2 boxes at a time and I would start in September when the Halloween displays would come out. I would continue to buy these boxes as the number of mini chocolate bars dwindled. After all, we had to make sure we had enough for when the kids arrived.

Then Halloween would finally come and we would get the same 16 kids we get every year. We would be left with well over 100 chocolate bars. This would tide us through until the Christmas chocolate boxes came out.

I am sure some of you can relate to these embarrassing stories of decadence, guilt and shame. So now I don't give out chocolate to anyone or buy it or keep it in the house. It is too much for me to resist and if I want to stay healthy and fit, chocolate is definitely off my shopping list.

So how do I replace that you may ask. By loving myself and the dear ones around me. If chocolate gives you the feeling of being in love, how about being in love? Treat yourself with love. Spoil yourself with a real treat. Fresh cut flowers, a spa day, a massage, a bubble bath, a weekend getaway. Be in love with who you are and what you have. Your self esteem will have improved greatly by following a superior plant-based diet. You don't want to give up this gift of great self love for something as mundane as a piece of chocolate.

Oil and Fats – 4,000 calories per pound

Finally, the granddaddy of calorie density. Oil comes in at 4,000 calories a pound. Sorry to say this also includes coconut oil. People claim it is very healthy, which it is somewhat. But the huge calorie amount negates any slight nutritional benefit one can get by eating it. And coconut oil has the added disadvantage as being a saturated fat. Saturated fat is great for clogging arteries.

If you want to lose weight, you do not want to add any kind of oil to your diet and your body doesn't need it. Every food even the innocent potato has some fat in it. But you say, oil tastes good! Fried things taste so good. Oil doesn't taste good. Have you ever drunk oil? It's nasty. You can get flavor without the fat and without adding sugar or salt to make up for it. You just have to retrain your tastebuds.

Oil is plain dangerous. It is molecularly unstable and must be stored carefully away from heat, light and air. Hence the dark glass bottles for your extra virgin organic olive oil. They are trying to give it a fighting chance to remain palatable before it goes rancid.

Kitchen clean up is super easy when you don't have slimy oil all over your dishes and cookware. There are no health advantages to adding oil to your diet. It's not like it will give you a nice shiny coat because you don't have a coat. Believe me, your body will use the fat on your body faster if you don't add it to your diet. Save your calories and fill your stomach with healthy satiating vegetables, fruits, grains and legumes.

I've touched on the dangers here but in the next chapter I will discuss the three 'foods' that keep you fat in more detail. I will also give you alternatives so that you can still get lots of delicious flavorful food without compromising your health and weight loss goals.

TASKS

1. This is more a passive exercise. Start thinking about all your favorite fruit, vegetables, grains and legumes. Think about what dishes that you can make featuring these foods.

2. When you go to the supermarket, have a look at the fruit and vegetables that are in season. These are usually the ones that are prominently featured. For example, in the Spring they feature asparagus. Summer is berries and all the stuff for beautiful salads. Fall is root vegetables and tree fruit. And Winter is squash and cruciferous vegetables.

Chapter Four

SOS FREE

Why We Want to Get Rid of Sugar, Oil and Salt

If you are obese you are a great candidate for acquiring metabolic syndrome. It sounds daunting but not as scary as the three diseases that make it up. Type 2 diabetes, cardiovascular disease and hypertension. If you are obese you are probably suffering from at least one of these and if you have all three, BINGO you win. This is metabolic syndrome.

So, what is the big contributing factor to these three illnesses? Obesity caused by the over consumption of sugar, oil and salt among other things. Now, you may be saying I don't eat very much of these things but the fact is that they are in everything that is processed.

Food manufacturers give millions of dollars to their laboratories. These labs find the right combination of ingredients to make their product irresistible. That special combination of sugar, oil and salt in the products. This combination sets off the addictive bliss point in our brains. It makes these products addictive. This isn't even including additives like MSG, food preservatives, and artificial favors.

Sugar

Let's start with sugar. So, what's so bad about it? Well, if you have been eating sugar for your entire life chances are you have some strong addictions to it. And it is in everything and has many names. Just like the devil. The tongue can detect even the smallest amount of sugar and it tastes like more.

Sugar may not be your go-to food trigger but I am sure if you are overweight somewhere in your big meal will be a lot of sugar. Soft drinks are loaded with sugar. If you read any food label, you will see the number of grams per serving of sugar. 4 grams equals 1 teaspoon of sugar. A 23-ounce can of Coca Cola is 39 grams of sugar. That's 9 1/3 teaspoons of sugar! So, you can imagine how much sugar you are consuming every day. When you do this day in and day out you start to show signs of wear and tear.

When you ingest sugar, it is the job of the pancreas to release insulin to neutralize it. If you eat a lot of refined sugar daily, the pancreas gets overworked. It can't keep up with the demand for insulin. This causes too much sugar to circulate in the blood causing high blood sugar readings. This is when you have high blood sugar. Your pancreas is doing its job providing as much insulin as it can. You are just eating too much sugar.

So, imagine you eat a big piece of sugary confection. The blood sugar rapidly increases and spikes. Then the pancreas releases a lot of insulin to counteract the threat to the body. This causes the blood sugar to drop very low. Then you to feel tired, cranky and hungry. You start getting serious food cravings. It makes the body seek out food to compensate for this low.

If the next thing you eat is processed food, it results in another big spike of blood sugar. Then followed by another big dump of insulin and back to a low level. And here come the cravings and agitation.

If this continues day in and day out for years what we have is a perpetually raised blood sugar level. At this point the doctor may put a person on metformin to help regulate the blood sugar spikes. Metformin helps reduce the absorption of sugar, which means that less sugar makes it into your bloodstream. If you continue to eat too much refined sugar, you will be on Metformin for the rest of your life.

The irony is that our cells need sugar for energy. But high sugar content coupled with a high-fat diet leads to reduced sensitivity to insulin. What happens is that the fat that is absorbed into the body plugs up the cells' signaling receptors. So, even though there is too much sugar in the blood, it can't get into the cells. The fat is blocking the way. This is called insulin resistance. It is an early stage of developing full blown Type 2 diabetes. Try eating a donut after reading that!

A low sugar diet is prescribed to get people off the roller coaster. But it rarely solves the problem. These diets incorporate sugar in the diet in the form of processed foods. It's like giving an alcoholic a teaspoon of alcohol every meal. Eventually, their addiction will be activated and there goes the low sugar diet.

How do we solve the problem? Total abstinence from sugar. Stop the blood sugar spikes. Stop the influx of sugar into the body. Sugar contains no fiber. Fiber is critical to slow down the release of sugar into the blood stream.

Fresh fruit is loaded with fiber. Fiber slows down the release time of sugar. Then the pancreas can do the appropriate amount of work to gently guide the blood sugar down to a healthy level. Can you see the difference between what a piece of fruit does to you blood sugar? So, eat your pound of fresh fruit every day to add that natural sweetness to your diet.

Blood sugar spikes are called sugar highs for a reason. They play with your brain chemistry in such a way as to give you tons of perceived euphoria and short-term energy. But when that blood sugar crashes, a sugar low, well all the euphoria is gone and with it the energy. Wouldn't it be better to have sustained happiness and energy all day long? That was how we were designed.

Let's look at sugar as a food trigger. When I would binge eat, sugar was never my first choice. I was a salt fiend but sugar would always be part of the binge at some point and I mean a lot of sugar! There was never enough chocolate or cookies to quench the craving. There was never enough sugar. Never. Once you get that sugar high you don't want to come down. It is a legal drug and it is killing people every day.

So, what do people with diabetes have to look forward to in the future? Well, I think everyone knows about the insulin injections. But what if you don't go to the doctor that often and this chronic high blood sugar and insulin resistance is not detected and you have become diabetic? What are the consequences of not taking care of your health through excellent nutrition or injecting insulin?

Long-term problems from diabetes are slow to develop. But the less controlled your blood sugar and fat intake the higher the risk of problems. Eventually, diabetes may be disabling or even life-threatening. There are several possible health problems from uncontrolled diabetes. These include cardiovascular disease, nerve damage, kidney damage and eye damage.

- Cardiovascular disease - If you have diabetes, you're more likely to have heart disease or a stroke.

- Nerve damage - Excess sugar can injure the walls of the tiny blood vessels that nourish your nerves. Especially in your legs. Nerve damage in the feet increases the risk of various foot infections which often do not heal well. This may result in toe, foot or leg amputation.

- Kidney damage - Kidneys contain millions of tiny blood vessels that filter waste from your blood. Diabetes can damage this delicate filtering system. Severe damage can lead to kidney failure or kidney disease.

- Eye damage - Diabetes can damage the blood vessels of the retina, potentially leading to blindness. Diabetes also increases the risk of cataracts and glaucoma.

Fresh or frozen fruit is great because the fiber slows down the delivery of the sugar in the bloodstream. If you do have a serious problem with blood sugar, choose fresh fruits

Although fresh fruit is good, avoid dried fruits. They are concentrated in both calories and sugar. For example: 1 cup of grapes is 110 calories, 1 cup of raisins is 646 calories. Raisins are incredibly calorie dense and so the sugar (the glycemic load) in the raisins is much higher.

On a glycemic load chart, the grape comes in at a respectable 11 for 120 grams. This is on the low end of the middle category. The raisin has a glycemic load of 28 for 60 grams. Half as many grams. It is the highest on the chart. So, for now keep all dried fruits out of the house. If you want some sugar, go for the grapes.

You may ask about sugar substitutes. They are in some cases even worse. Aspartame has been known to cause cancer in rats. By eating a sugar substitute, you are attempting to trick your brain and body that sugar is around. You can't trick your body and you may end up having massive sugar cravings as a result.

The same is true for stevia. If you are not eating the actual leaves don't use any highly processed powder to get the sweetness you desire. It is the same as an artificial sweetener which may trigger you to overeat or worse yet eat off plan. It's a slippery slope so stick to fresh and frozen delicious nutrient-dense fruit. You don't have to eat it all alone you can add fruit to your oatmeal or bake an oat and fruit-based dessert.

Oil

As I mentioned before oil is the granddaddy of calorie density at 4000 calories a pound. You are going to say so what. I am not going to drink a pound of it. But it is in everything. A quarter cup is approximately 500 calories. Anything fried will be adding to your oil total. Oil is used on almost everything in restaurants to add texture or to keep foods from sticking like rice and pasta. Why add something so unnecessary to your diet which has no nutritional value? If it is heated it can be dangerous to your health. Fried foods cause inflammation and accelerate the aging of the cells. And it packs on the calories.

One of the reasons I decided to become a vegan was to lower my cholesterol. It was super high and I felt I was at risk of heart disease like my mom and dad. Or at least on a statin medication to lower it like my sister and brother. I was determined not to be put on a medication that once prescribed is almost impossible to get off of. So, the easiest thing to do was to cut out animal products. All animals produce and store cholesterol, including humans. I didn't need to take in more of it by eating it. I was making enough of my own.

So, I became a vegan and my numbers went down somewhat but my vegan diet was not perfect. I ate all kinds of fatty vegan junk foods. French fries, spring rolls, and vegan dressings. Processed junk foods like chips and tortilla chips. Faux sour cream, faux cheeses and meats. Cookies, cakes and treats prepared with vegan margarine, coconut oil, palm oil or other oils.

When I was on point with my diet, I still used coconut oil for baking and popcorn. And I prepared dressings with olive or grapeseed oil. Vegetable dishes were still made with oil because after all it all comes from plants. I was so careful to store them properly too. No wonder I couldn't lose weight. I was easily consuming an extra 500 - 1000 calories in fat per day.

Let's look at two dangerous plant-based oils. My beloved coconut oil is about 90% saturated fat. It is a higher percentage than butter (about 64% saturated fat), beef fat (40%), or even lard (also 40%). I used it in and on everything. I even bought that giant container from Costco just for me.

Palm oil is about 50% saturated fat. It is cheap so a lot of processed food manufacturers use it. It can be found in a lot of processed foods. These include cereals, baked goods, protein bars, diet bars, chocolate, and margarine. Palm oil is also added to some nut butters as a stabilizer. This prevents the oil from separating and settling at the top of the jar.

Saturated fats are bad for your health especially for the heart. Too much saturated fat can cause cholesterol to build up in your arteries. Also, saturated fats raise your LDL (bad) cholesterol. No wonder I couldn't get my cholesterol and triglycerides under control.

I was oblivious to the fact that I was undermining my health and my weight loss by incorporating these 'healthy' plant-based fats.

If you want to stay away from a weigh and measure program, definitely stay away from oil. You can fry anything using a little water or broth and get the same results. You can bake on parchment paper so you don't need to grease anything. You can also bake using silicone bakeware and nothing sticks to it. The latest gadget is an air fryer. You get nice crisp fries and vegetables without any oil whatsoever.

You can adapt your other recipes to be oil free as well. For example, I use white beans to create creamy dressings and sauces. I replace the oil in my salad dressings with water. I will add a tablespoon of ground flax seeds or chia seeds for some healthy Omega 3 fat. These seeds also help to thicken the dressing like an oil would without the unhealthy calories.

When I air fry potatoes or other vegetables, I brush them with aquafaba. Aquafaba sounds fancy. But it is just the water from canned or boiled chickpeas or other beans. Then I sprinkle no-salt seasoning on the vegetables so the seasoning will stick to them. Delicious and oil free.

Salt

Salt consumption is linked to hypertension. When you eat too much salt, your body tries to dilute it by retaining water. This places pressure on the blood vessels and leads to high blood pressure. Over time, your vessels eventually weaken, making it hard for the blood to flow through. So, if you have high blood pressure you are contributing to your risk of heart disease and stroke.

Salt is inflammatory. It does damage to the delicate epithelial cells inside your veins and arteries. When these are damaged your LDL cholesterol comes along and patches up the holes. It's like a road crew doing patchwork on a road. The continuous progressive damage and repair can lead to blocked veins and arteries. High blood pressure represents how hard your heart is working to pump blood all over your body. Salt also affects the kidneys which is an organ that helps to regulate blood pressure.

Salt is a food trigger. And boy do I know about this. Salt highjacks your tastebuds. So, something that isn't salted seems bland and boring by comparison. Salty snacks were my favorite binge food. Chips, crackers, popcorn anything with tons of salt was much more delicious to me.

In my studies, I have read tons on the dangers of salt in the diet and that you should limit it to ideally 1,500 mg per day. But when you are in denial with a salt addiction, you add it to everything you cook and maybe again when you serve it. That's a problem and seriously over the recommended 1,500 mg per day. By the way, 2,300 mg of sodium is equal to about 1 teaspoon of salt. And like sugar it is in everything! Can you imagine how much hidden sodium you are consuming in a day. That's even before you pick up the salt shaker.

Besides that, when you salt your food, you can eat a lot more of it. This means one bowl of healthy chili leads to two bowls because it tastes so darn good. Or maybe even three. Then you have tripled your calorie intake for the meal and are not going to lose that extra weight.

One of the things that I learned from Chef AJ was that it takes 30 days for your tastebuds to adapt to a no-salt diet. I would always give up long before this time. The easiest way to do this is to go to a retreat for water fasting for a few weeks to totally reprogram your taste buds. But for most people that is not workable or affordable.

The alternative is to remove the sodium from your recipes. Or choose recipes that do not contain salt. Start using products like Mrs. Dash or Kirkland Organic No Salt Seasoning to replace the salt. Double up on your spices and herbs in the recipes. Add seaweed or kelp powder to your soups. Add celery to your soups and stews. Add an acid like vinegar or lemon or lime juice to finish your soups and stews.

If you still can't choke down the food and you do not suffer from high blood pressure, add a little salt to your dish. You should measure it if you have to use it so you don't use too much. Make sure you increase your water intake by at least a couple of glasses to flush out the excess sodium.

The thing about salt and weight loss is that it makes food taste delicious and hence you will eat a lot more of it. If you have to add a little salt in any form, make sure that you don't go back for seconds of your delicious starches. I am giving you a pass on this only if you can't eat the meal without salt and are in danger of giving up this new way of eating entirely. But by cutting out salt completely, your health will improve. And your tastebuds will adapt to the actual flavors of the foods.

The next chapter is probably the most critical in ensuring your weight loss success. It won't be easy but it is so freeing. Enjoy the process.

Chapter Five

Clean Environment = Clean Eating

Okay the next thing that you will be taking care of is quite a daunting task. As a matter of fact, I dedicate an entire chapter to it. But of all the things in this book, it is one of the most critical steps. I feel that this alone will ensure your success. It worked for me.

Chef AJ says 'you don't have to be perfect if your environment is.' It is all about the kitchen clean out, meal planning and shopping. The next chapter deals with bulk cooking but first we have to set ourselves up for success. You want all the bad food out and all the good healthy food in prepped and ready to go. Then you won't be tempted to eat things that you are addicted to or will not serve you in reaching your goal weight. Here's two other Chef AJ sayings on the subject. Choose your favorite and make it your new mantra. 'You don't need willpower to not eat something that isn't there.' Or how about, 'preparation trumps motivation.'

Kitchen Clean Out

Now is the time to get serious. It is said that the Vikings would burn their boats when they arrived in a new land so that they couldn't back track and had to make a go of it. It's time to burn your boat. Clean out your kitchen. This is a great opportunity to do some Spring cleaning.

So, when you are cleaning out your kitchen you are going to go through everything. You are going to have 3 categories. Throw away, give away and keepers.

Throw Away

The first category is things that you are going to throw away. This includes all processed foods that have been opened or partially used. Toss them if they contain **oil, sugar, additives, fat, chemicals, wheat flour, and salt**. So, anything that is not found in nature. Sorry, there are no nacho chip trees out there.

Let's start in the cabinets. Check the expiry date on all your canned and bottled goods. If they have expired definitely toss them. All open bags are tossed if they contain the oil, sugar, wheat flour or salt.

Give Away

Next put aside items that you know are definitely not on your food list but are sealed and perfectly good. These items you will be donating or giving them away to friends or family.

No one reads labels. This will require a lot of label reading so grab your glasses. If there are more than 5 ingredients on the list you probably will be tossing it. Flour, sugar, noodles, pastas, chocolate in all forms and the usual baking goodies all have to go. Nuts, seeds, oils, nut butters, all have to go. Mac and cheese, baked beans with sugar in the ingredients, canned soups with salt, etc.

Keepers

Finally, you have the items left that you are going to keep. This includes whole grains, legumes, chia, flax and hemp seeds and all salt-free spices and herbs. It also includes canned tomatoes, tomato sauce and tomato paste. Make sure there is no added salt. Keep all types of vinegars. But white vinegar is for cleaning not for eating.

Fridge and Freezer

In the freezer, you will know what has to be given away and thrown away. Any dairy or non-dairy ice-cream like products. Premade dinners, pizzas, any food triggers that are hiding in there. You will know what they are.

In the fridge, here's a chance to really make some room. You are keeping all fresh fruits and vegetables. You are getting rid of all condiments that contain salt, sugar or oil. Sadly, the ketchup has to go and I even had to give my neighbors some perfect avocados with a tear in my eye. I remember it like it was yesterday. Keep your mustards; yellow, Dijon, and seeded. All will help add flavor to your meals and dressings.

This is like pulling off a band aid. The sooner that you get rid of all the highly processed foods and trigger foods the better. Your kitchen will become a safe place.

Don't forget to take this opportunity to wipe down your cabinets and fridge. Get ready for all the beautiful healthy foods you will be stocking it up with.

I know that in some cases this can be a very difficult process. For me, I am blessed with a lot of space. I had a few big storage bins that I could 'hide' some food in until I was ready to give it to my friend. I also had a second fridge/freezer in the basement that I could store things in until I saw her.

Getting rid of the expired food was a no brainer. But the food that was really tough for me was pasta. I love pasta and I bought only the best brown rice pasta I could find. I have always intended to reintroduce some pasta into my diet at some point but I have yet to do it. I find that I get just as much enjoyment of putting my favorite Italian inspired sauce over rice.

Obviously, the pasta had to go. It was a huge trigger for me. I could eat a whole package on my own which is impressive, scary and very sad all at the same time. Ask yourself the old question. If you were on a deserted island and could only bring one food with you, which food would it be? Chances are it is loaded with calories and a huge food trigger for you. Mine was a toss up between pasta or popcorn. So even my beloved organic popcorn kernels had to go in the box. Along with all coconut products; coconut milk, coconut butter, and coconut oil. It is loaded with fat including saturated fat and there is no way to lose weight with that in your kitchen.

Safe Storage Containers

Okay…. now that your kitchen is pretty much bare let's talk about storage containers. You are going to need a lot of them.

Although BPA free plastic containers are acceptable, I prefer glass containers for everything. I have included a checklist of storage containers you will need. (Appendix 4) This is what I have but you can work up to this and use what you have until you can get them all.

Starting with the fridge, you need some small, medium and large mason jars. They are used to store homemade dressings and sauces. Also, buy 2 large rectangular glass cake pans and 2 small square glass cake pans all with silicone lids (I use Anchor brand).

The large ones are for your mixed greens and spinach. Line the bottoms with paper towels. Fill with your greens and place a paper towel on top which will soak up any additional moisture from the greens. It makes it easier to grab handfuls of greens. They will last the entire week stored this way without rotting. If you can't fit all the greens in at one time that's fine. Just make sure you put a paper towel on the top of the greens in the clamshell before you put it back in the fridge. This will help to suck up the extra moisture.

The small square glass containers are for your fresh herbs like cilantro and parsley. I have one for each. Do the same method of lining the container with paper towel. Place in the herbs, make sure you undo any elastics that keep them tight together and I cut off the stems. Also make sure they are packed loosely in the container. Top with another piece of paper towel and store in the fridge. Herbs stored this way will last 1 – 2 weeks if you haven't eaten them all by then.

You will also need at least 2 big glass bowls with silicon lids. You can buy these in sets of 3 with large, medium, and small bowls in a set. I use these for my prepared salad ingredients like cucumber, carrots, and celery. The other one I use for tabouleh. This is a combination of quinoa, chickpeas and other ingredients. It is a perfect starch to add to my salad.

Now we come to the fridge and freezer storage containers. You can buy these in sets of 3 - 5 depending on the size. They come in 1-cup, 2-cup and 4-cup serving sizes. The fewest you'll need will be the 1 cup size. as I use them mostly for dry ingredients or individual servings of sauces or hummus. I have at least 15 of the 2-cup sizes. It is the perfect size for individual portions of chile and stews. The 4-cup sizes I reserve for soups and rice. These containers freeze well and this is how I store my prepared foods in the freezer.

The next thing you need is large BPA free freezer bags. You can use these for so many things. Freezing overripe bananas for nice cream. Freezing beans that you have precooked. To keep costs down it is cost effective to cook big quantities of beans and freeze them in one big bag. When you want to thaw expose the beans from the bag and run them under hot water. Then you can thaw just the amount that you need for your recipe and put the rest back in the freezer. I use another bag for vegetable peelings and ends from when I prep my other vegetables. I use these peelings to make broth.

The other item that I just love is more of a buy-as-you-go item. I buy the big glass storage jars that you can get at the dollar store. It makes all your dry goods easily accessible rather than piles of plastic bags. I use them for beans, lentils, quinoa, chia, dates, and more. It makes it easier to take inventory of what you need more of when you are making your shopping list. And they look gorgeous with all the different colors of beans and lentils.

APPENDIX 4: STORAGE CONTAINER SHOPPING LIST

MASON JARS

- 4 extra large jars for soaking beans (holds 8 cups)
- 3 large jars for dressings and sauces (holds 4 cups)
- 3 medium jars for dressings and sauces (holds 2 cups)

BIG STUFF

- 2 large rectangular glass cake pans with lids – for mixed greens/spinach
- 2 small square glass cake pans with lids – cilantro/parsley/other herbs
- 2 big glass bowls with lids – for salad vegetables/tabouleh (I bought these in sets of 3 – large/medium/small. The other bowls are a bonus and come in handy.)

GLASS STORAGE CONTAINERS WITH SILICON LIDS

- 6 – 1 cup size – I use for individual hummus portions/ ground flax/extra dressings/leftovers
- 15 – 2 cup size. This what I put all my chilis, curries and stews in and freeze in individual meal portions. I also use it for hummus.
- 12 – 4 cup size. I use these for soups, rice and grains, and cooked vegetables.

BPA Free Large Freezer Bags – I use these for freezing ripe bananas, cooked beans, applesauce, fruit, and veggie ends and peelings to make broth. I also use them to store my baked potatoes in the fridge.

*OPTIONAL – Glass storage jars for beans, lentils, rice, and other grains. I get mine at the dollar store. They are really pretty and helps you keep track of inventory.

Menu Planning

Next, we are going to talk about meal plans. It is useful to have your days planned out in advance. Working without a meal plan is like going into battle without a plan. If you go shopping without a list you may forget ingredients or buy things you don't need. That means more money!

We need to have your Goal Book with the skeletons of your daily menu plans on hand. You need a small notepad for a shopping list. And some recipes that you want to make for the week. See Appendix 5 for a sample menu plan for my typical week. This overview plan is what I would put in my Goal Book for each day of the upcoming week.

Your first breakfast will be vegetables. I love a giant fresh chopped salad for breakfast. It gets in my vegetable quota for my target sheet and kills my cravings for the day. If the weather is cold you can opt for steamed vegetables or vegetable soup. Chef AJ says, 'if you are not hungry enough to eat vegetables, you aren't really hungry.'

So, for my breakfast for 7 days most of my ingredients are fresh and will have to be purchased every week. I add on my shopping list 2 large clamshells of greens. One of spinach and the other of mixed greens. Then I add a bunch of low starch vegetables and a small handful of chopped cilantro or other herb to my salad. This adds some interesting flavor and boosts my nutrition. Then I add about 1 cup of tabouleh which is made with quinoa and chickpeas. It adds some interesting elements to the salad. and the starch keeps me satisfied much longer. I finish with a salt and oil free dressing or drizzle some balsamic vinegar on top and I am ready to go.

Second breakfast will be a satisfying and usually an oat-based breakfast. Like a large oat square, oatmeal with fresh fruit, oatmeal cookies all without sugar, oil or salt. I usually bake a square or something with oats on the weekend and it will last the entire week.

Lunch is usually potato or sweet potato based. Like a big baked potato with cheez sauce and another vegetable on the side. Like steamed broccoli, cauliflower, a slaw salad or another type of salad.

Anytime you want you will be eating a pound of fresh fruit so it is totally up to you when you want to get this in. But make sure that you make note of it on your meal plan and shop accordingly. I usually buy at least 7 apples, 7 oranges, a bunch of bananas, and a seasonal fruit. I always buy bananas and freeze what I don't eat. When they get too ripe, they come in handy for baking and for making nice cream. I like to buy oranges and apples because they don't go bad in a week so I know that I'll always have fruit on hand.

Dinner is usually bean and rice based. Whatever kind of soup, stew or chili I make I serve it over rice. This makes the meal super satisfying. I like to start my meal with either a salad or veggies and hummus. I then move on to the beans and rice. This satiates my hunger and ensures that I am eating the more calorie dense foods last. After dinner, I do the dishes and the kitchen is closed. This gives me plenty of time to start the digestion process before bed.

I want to point out that you will be eating a wet starch three or four times each and every day. Do NOT restrict your wet starches. This is critical if you want to lose weight. If you eat enough wet starch at your meals, you will not be hungry between meals or after dinner. So, make sure you do not skimp of the wet starches like oatmeal, potatoes, rice and beans. These are the foods that will keep you satisfied and you will not be so hungry as to bring on a binge.

It was easy to tell when I wasn't on a diet in the past. I wouldn't prepare a menu plan for the following week. I wouldn't make a shopping list. I would buy what I felt like. I wouldn't know what I would be making so I wouldn't have time to prepare and cook. That meant highly processed food from the supermarket.

Or I would come home so tired from the work day. The last thing that I wanted to do was to spend another hour making dinner. That's where take out becomes so much easier and dangerous. Meal planning ensures that you are hitting all your daily targets. It keeps you on track to your goal.

APPENDIX 5: SAMPLE MENU PLAN

	MONDAY	TUESDAY	WENESDAY	THURSDAY
BREAKFAST	BIG SALAD (GREENS, MIXED VEGGIES, QUINIOA TABBOULEH, BALSAMIC VINEGAR)	BIG SALAD (GREENS, MIXED VEGGIES, QUINIOA TABBOULEH, BALSAMIC VINEGAR)	BIG SALAD (GREENS, MIXED VEGGIES, QUINIOA TABBOULEH, BALSAMIC VINEGAR)	BIG SALAD (GREENS, MIXED VEGGIES, QUINIOA TABBOULEH, BALSAMIC VINEGAR)
2ND BREAKFAST	APPLE CRUMBLE & FRESH FRUIT	APPLE CRUMBLE & FRESH FRUIT	APPLE CRUMBLE & FRESH FRUIT	APPLE CRUMBLE & FRESH FRUIT
LUNCH	BIG BAKED POTATO WITH CHEEZY SAUCE ROASTED BRUSSELS SPROUTS	BIG BAKED POTATO WITH CHEEZY SAUCE STEAMED BROCCOLI	BIG BAKED POTATO WITH CHEEZY SAUCE ROASTED BRUSSELS SPROUTS	BIG BAKED POTATO WITH CHEEZY SAUCE STEAMED BROCCOLI
DINNER	3 BEAN CHILI RICE VEGGIES & HUMMUS	GREEN LENTIL CURRY RICE VEGGIES & HUMMUS	3 BEAN CHILI RICE VEGGIES & HUMMUS	GREEN LENTIL CURRY RICE VEGGIES & HUMMUS

Note: Obviously, this menu will continue for the full week. The only changes are alternating vegetables for lunch and alternating entrees for dinner. You can print off the 7-day sample menu plan and the blank menu plan template on my website: www.karenwarwickrhn.com.

Shopping

Now your kitchen is nice and clean and empty! You have your food storage containers. You have done your menu planning and shopping list. (See Appendix 6 for a sample shopping list based on the sample meal plan.) Time to get some food. This shopping trip will be unlike any other that you have made. I can clearly remember before I began to eat this way, I would buy an entire cart full of processed foods. All cans and packages. I would throw in a few apples just so that the cashier wouldn't think I wasn't a total food loser.

Of course, I would never eat those apples. I would wait until they were liquified in the bag somewhere in the bottom of the crisper. There were always more interesting foods to eat. But now things are different and you won't believe how absurdly proud you will be of yourself. All this healthy food in your cart! It will give you some self confidence knowing that everything in your cart is good for you.

I have included a list of what I buy in a weekly shopping trip. This list is for one person so make adjustments if you are shopping for your family. You would need to make a list based off of the recipes that you have chosen. Also include the snacking fruit and salad vegetables you prefer. This list is in appendix 6.

When you get your shopping bags home this is a critical time. Don't put those vegetables in the crisper drawer to wilt and die. Have you ever seen what happens to radish leaves after a couple of days in a plastic bag? I have. You want to start your washing and prep work as soon as you can. It doesn't make any difference how many vegetables you buy if you don't eat them. You want to make them as easily accessible as possible. So put your greens and herbs in their proper containers. Don't forget the paper towel.

When you open the fridge, you want to have all your fixings for a meal within grasp. All the prep work is done. I slice and chop all my salad vegetables except for my greens (which I store in the glass containers) as soon as I get home. That way I have a giant bowl of salad vegetables ready. It takes me 5 minutes to throw a delicious salad together once this is done.

APPENDIX 6: SHOPPING LIST BASED ON THE SAMPLE MENU PLAN

VEGETABLES	BEANS (IN SMALL CANS OR DRY IF YOU HAVE TIME)
• 1 LARGE CLAMSHELL SPINACH • 1 LARGE CLAMSHELL MIXED GREENS • CILANTRO • CUCUMBER (2-3) • CARROTS • BABY CARROTS • CELERY • SWEET BELL PEPPERS 4 • GREEN ONION • RADISHES • TOMATOES • 1 RED ONION • 2 LARGE YELLOW OR WHITE ONIONS • PARSLEY	• 2 CANS CHICK PEAS/GARBANZO BEANS • 2 CUPS DRY NAVY (WHITE) BEANS • 2 CUPS DRY GREEN LENTILS • 1 CAN BLACK BEANS • 1 CAN KIDNEY BEANS • 1 CAN PINTO BEANS SPICES & CONDIMENTS • APPLE CIDER VINEGAR • BALSAMIC VINEGAR • BAY LEAVES

• 4 GIANT RUSSET POTATOES OR A BAG OF MEDIUM SIZED. • FRESH OR FROZEN BROCCOLI • 1-2 LBS. BRUSSELS SPROUTS FRUIT • 12 LEMONS (at least) • 7 ORANGES • 12 APPLES • 4 LARGE GRANNY SMITH APPLES • 7 BANANAS • ANOTHER FUN FRUIT GRAINS • QUINOA • ROLLED OATS • BROWN LONG GRAIN RICE	• CHILI POWDER • CINNAMON • CUMIN • CURRY POWDER • DIJON MUSTARD • GARLIC POWDER • GINGER • ITALIAN HERBS (NO SALT) • ONION POWDER • NUTRITIONAL YEAST (at least 2 cups) • PEPPER • RED THAI CURRY PASTE • TURMERIC • MRS DASH NO SALT SEASONING OR ANOTHER OTHER • ORGANIC UNSWEETENED APPLE JUICE • UNSWEETENED APPLE SAUCE • 1 LARGE CAN NO SALT DICED TOMATOES

Fresh

The big question will be 'do I have to buy organic everything?' The answer is no unless you have big piles of money. There are some products that are known to be highly sprayed with pesticides so it is always good to buy organic. But if you can't afford it, wash the produce very well. You can also cut off the area at the stem where the pesticide liquid could gather and dry. I do this for peppers that are scary expensive if they are organic.

Fruits that have thick skins like oranges and bananas don't need to be organic as the skin protects the fruit. Vegetables that you peel anyway don't necessarily need to be organic either.

Here's the 'dirty dozen' list of the fruits and vegetables you should always try to buy organic. These crops use a lot of pesticides.

Here are the fruits on the dirty dozen list: apples, blueberries, cherries, grapes, nectarines, peaches and strawberries.

Here are the vegetables on the dirty dozen list: celery, cucumber, leafy greens (all), potatoes, tomatoes, and sweet bell peppers.

Farm markets are another option for getting fresh produce and they are always fun to visit. Some areas have delivery services for local organic vegetables. You can order online and have them delivered weekly right to your door.

Frozen

Frozen fruit and vegetables are handy to have when you are in a hurry. Frozen berries are cost efficient out of season. Frozen broccoli and cauliflower are also cost efficient. They are already cleaned, stemmed and ready to cook. It's a super easy and fast way to incorporate a lot more vegetables into your diet without a lot of prep work. There are even interesting mixes available.

Canned, Dried Goods and Cool Storage

Canned goods are pretty reasonably priced. You will be eating a lot of different kinds of beans. The most common varieties can be found in your supermarket. It is not the cheapest way to go but it is definitely the most convenient.

Also, make sure to check the sodium content in canned beans. I try to have a stock pile of two of each variety in my pantry. These are great for last minute cooking ideas. They are convenient when I have low motivation for extensive cooking. A can of beans can be added to a giant salad or thrown into almost any dish to add protein and carbohydrates. This helps to make a meal more satisfying and filling.

I also have canned diced tomatoes; tomato sauce and tomato paste all salt free and organic. Costco in my town has cases for sale at very reasonable prices.

Dried Goods

This includes all your dried legumes, quinoa, rolled oats, and varieties of rice. I pour them from the plastic bags into my big glass jars as they are more accessible and I always know how much I have left.

Cool Storage

This is a place for your potatoes, sweet potatoes, onions, garlic, shallots and ginger. I have a cupboard reserved for this. I put the potatoes and sweet potatoes in one basket and the onions and smaller stuff in the other. I usually leave my squashes out on the kitchen table. They are pretty and it encourages me to use them up rather than hiding them in a dark cupboard.

Now that your kitchen is totally clean, it is time to get cooking. The next chapter breaks down the whole process. Get ready to cook!

TASKS

1. Do your kitchen clean out. Do it as quickly and efficiently as you can. You don't want to draw out this process. As soon as your environment is clean, you will be ready to start.

2. Make sure you have enough storage containers at home before you go shopping. You don't want your healthy fruit and vegetables hidden in bags. That never works. Also you want your containers for storing your prepped meals. So, if you are using what I recommend or making do with what you have, just make sure you have enough.

3. Make your meal plan and shopping list for the week.

4. Do your shopping for the week and put what you can away in its proper container. Our next chapter is Bulk Cooking. So now we are finally getting serious.

Chapter Six

Keep It Simple – Bulk Cooking

The easiest way to stay on track with this diet is through bulk cooking. You want to cook for the entire week so that you have a stock pile of compliant food that is all ready to go. It is in our human nature to avoid pain, seek pleasure and do it as efficiently as possible. Drive through restaurants have this figured out. They provide cheap food as fast as possible. It's also extremely unhealthy food. I can hardly call it food.

Our goal with bulk cooking for the week is to play upon these principles. To make our delicious compliant food as fast and as pleasurable as possible to eat. Who knows what the week will bring? What fires you will have to put out? Being prepared is an essential key to success.

So, let's get started. The plan that I have set forth is what I do in a typical week. It usually takes 3 days to get everything done for the week but you might be more efficient than I am. I have included only a few recipes as this is not a cookbook. You can find tons of recipes in the books by Chef AJ, Dr. Caldwell Esselstyn, Rip Esselstyn, and Dr. John McDougall. Also, check out their websites. There is no shortage of healthful compliant recipes. These recipes will help reach your goals of weight loss and excellent health.

Equipment

I am a self-confessed gadget queen. My husband never has to worry about what to get me for Christmas or my birthday. I always have a list ready of the latest gadgets that I want. But not everyone has my weakness so I will take that into consideration and give you some options.

I also took a knife skills course where the vegan chef said that all you need is a good knife and cutting board. That's a little too minimalistic for me. I have provided a basic list of the equipment that I use every week in Appendix 7.

APPENDIX 7: COOKING EQUIPMENT

BASIC EQUIPMENT	APPLIANCES & DEVICES
<ul><li>CHEF'S KNIFE</li><li>SERATED KNIFE</li><li>CUTTING BOARD</li><li>VEGETABLE PEELER</li><li>BIG STEAL SPOON</li><li>BIG SLOTTED SPOON</li><li>2 LARGE LIDDED BOWLS</li><li>1 LARGE MIXING BOWL</li><li>DRY MEASURE CUPS</li><li>WET MEASURE CUPS</li><li>MEASURING SPOONS</li><li>FINE MESH STRAINER</li><li>A SPATULA</li><li>A VEGGIE STEAMER</li></ul> OTHER STUFF <ul><li>BRITA OR BERKEY WATER FILTER</li><li>A CITRUS JUICER (SOMETHING LOW</li></ul>	<ul><li>HIGH POWERED BLENDER</li><li>A STOVE TOP</li><li>AN OVEN</li><li>AN INSTAPOT (OPTIONAL)</li><li>AN AIR FRYER (OPTIONAL)</li><li>A RICE COOKER (OPTIONAL)</li></ul> COOKWARE <ul><li>1 COOKIE SHEET</li><li>1 COVERED BAKING DISH</li><li>2 LARGE POTS (FOR CHILI & CURRY)</li><li>1 MEDIUM POT (FOR RICE)</li><li>1 SMALL POT (FOR QUINOA)</li></ul>

TECH FOR LEMON JUICE) • SALAD SPINNER (FOR ROMAINE LETTUCE OR NON-PREWASHED LETTUCE)	

Benefits of Bulk Cooking

Bulk cooking saves time. You don't have to think of what you are going to have for breakfast, lunch or dinner. It is waiting for you in the fridge or freezer. This way you will not be tempted to eat something that is off plan.

Things are going to get tough at work. Some days you are going to be running late to get home. Other days you will be so tired that the thought of cooking is out of the question. There is nothing better than just having to heat and serve your meal when you get home. The freezer is stocked with at least 2 different soup or stew options. Or you can heat up a baked potato and veggies in the microwave. Dinner in 3 minutes. Take that Door Dash!

Prep for 7 Days

This plan is based off the menu plan in this book but whatever you decide to make there will be some basics. I usually start on a Friday after work and am done by Sunday. You can also divide the tasks over the week. An hour per day ought to do it. But initially I want you to get off to a good start with the fridge and freezer totally stocked.

When you see your supplies of food dwindling, it is time to prepare that item again. For example, I find that I have to prepare the salad vegetables twice a week to have enough. Also, things like dressings and sauces can last a week and a half so you don't have to wait for the weekend to do your cooking. But initially to help keep yourself compliant, I urge you to have it all done before you start.

FRIDAY (DAY 1)

Set 2 cups of dry white (navy) beans in filtered water and a little apple cider vinegar to soak overnight. If you are using a big pot or an Instapot you can soak right in the pot. I soak my beans in big Mason jars so that they don't take up counter space.

Optional: You can soak your other beans that you will be using for chili and soups now. But to make this easy, use canned beans and chickpeas for the first week. Unless you have an Instapot. Then have at it.

SATURDAY (DAY 2)

- Cook and cool the pre-soaked navy beans (for Cheez Sauce)
- Make 3-Bean Chili. Cool and freeze in 2-cup containers.
- Make Green Lentil Curry. Cool and freeze in 2-cup containers. (If you only have one big pot you can do this on Sunday.)
- Bake potatoes (cool and store in a big Ziploc bag in the fridge)
- Cook rice, let cool, store in 4-cup containers. Freeze 2 but keep 1 in the fridge.

- Cook quinoa, let cool, store in 4-cup container. Keep in fridge until tomorrow.
- Make cheez sauce. Store in medium glass jars in the fridge.

SUNDAY (DAY 3)

- Make and bake apple crumble. Let cool and store in fridge.
- Prep and bake Brussel sprouts. Let cool and store in a 4-cup container in the fridge. (Or   steam vegetables at meal time if you prefer.)
- Make Tabouleh – make and store the Tabouleh in a big bowl with a lid and store in fridge.
- Prep salad vegetables – also prep into a big bowl with a lid and store in fridge.
- Make hummus – store in a 2-cup container in the fridge.
- Make dressing – if you are making a dressing now is the time to do it. If not make sure you have some balsamic vinegar on hand to dress your salad.

Preparing Your Salad Vegetables

After your shopping trip you should have your greens and herbs stored properly. Make sure that they are in their glass containers with paper towel lining. This is so they won't rot for the week that you will be using them. It also makes it fast to prepare your salad.

Now we are going to make a big bowl of salad vegetables that you keep separate from your greens. I keep them separate for two reasons:

1. If the greens and salad are mixed together it will be a smaller serving that you will be eating. You want to eat a pound of salad for breakfast. So, these heavier vegetables will help ensure that your salad is heavy enough.

2. Also, over the week you want to ensure that your salad keeps fresh and doesn't get too soggy. You don't want your last salad in the bowl to be a watery mess. That's not too appetizing.

Here is a step-by-step plan for making my salad vegetables to ensure this doesn't happen:

1. I start with 2 cucumbers. I peel and end the cucumbers and cut them in half. I cut the halves length ways and then into quarters. Then I deseed/jelly them by first cutting off the jelly part. After I cut this out there is still some seeds and jelly remaining. So I run a spoon down the length of the cucumber (bowl down) like hollowing out a canoe. After that, I roll up these four quarters in paper towel to get rid of the excess water. I continue the process until both cucumbers are done. Once the paper towels have absorbed the extra water, I dice the cucumbers and put them in the bowl.

2. I then wash, end and chop 2 celery stalks. I peel, end and chop 2 carrots. I wash, end, gut out the seeds of a large bell pepper. I end and slice 4 radishes and end and slice 2 or 3 green onions. I put the lid on and store in the fridge. This is enough to make about 5 or 6 salads. I use a 2-cup container to measure out my vegetables for my salad.

Assembling the Salad

This is how I make my breakfast salad. I use a big bowl

with a lid. Mine is stainless steel so I can take it to work.

1. I start with 2 big handfuls of spinach and chop them up on the cutting board. You can squeeze them down in a ball to chop them effectively. This is to save room in the bowl as chopped greens take up less space. Chopped greens are also more bioavailable for the body to break down.

2. Then I chop 2 big handfuls of mixed greens.

3. Then add a small handful of chopped cilantro or parsley is chopped stems and all.

4. Then my 2 cups of salad vegetables are added.

5. Then 1 heaping half cup of Quinoa Tabouleh is added. I include the recipe in this chapter. 6. When I am ready to eat it, I will add the dressing or balsamic vinegar. If you add the dressing a long time before you eat it, it can get soggy.

BALSAMIC DIJON ROASTED BRUSSELS SPROUTS
By Dr. Roy Artal

Ingredients:

- 1-2 lbs. of Brussels Sprouts
- ¼ cup balsamic vinegar
- ¼ cup Dijon mustard

1. Cut off end, halve or quarter Brussels sprouts, discard loose leaves and put in a large bowl.

2. Whisk together balsamic vinegar and Dijon mustard.

3. Pour mixture over the sprouts and mix to coat them.

4. Preheat oven to 400 degrees.

5. Line a cookie sheet with parchment paper.

6. Pour out the sprouts onto the cookie sheet and spread them out to ensure even cooking.

7. Bake for 30 minutes.

8. Remove from the oven and let cool.

9. Store in a 4-cup container in the fridge.

10. These are good hot or cold. I usually serve them as a side dish to my baked potato.

No Waste Kitchen

You are going to be eating a lot of vegetables every day. To get the most for your money, you want to try for a no waste kitchen. I take the ends and peelings from my salad and I freeze them in a large freezer bag. This I use as a base for a broth for soups, stews and chilis. For example, when I buy fresh broccoli for steamed vegetables, I am mostly eating the florets. I will chop and freeze the stalks to put in my big freezer bag.

Also, if your spinach is starting to turn, freeze that as well in a separate bag. The leaves freeze pretty flat and you can grab a frozen handful and chop to add to soups and stews or to your broth.

When you are eating so much fresh produce you want to make sure it is appealing for you to eat. If it isn't at its freshest, freeze it and replace it with fresher stuff. Then it won't go to waste. Before your next trip to the supermarket, you want to eat, cook, or freeze your produce before you restock it. This way your fridge stays clean and organized and you don't have to wonder what has died in your crisper drawer.

The same goes for fruit. Bananas are a great example. Always buy bananas. Once they get too ripe to eat, remove the skins and freeze flat in a freezer bag. I use them a lot for baking and for nice cream.

Apples are the same. They never have to die in your crisper. You can peel, core and freeze. Make them into a dessert or boil them down into apple sauce which can be used as a binder in baking.

Dressings and Sauces

I am including a recipe for Delicious Dressing as a demonstration. This is how you can make a dressing complaint without oil, salt or sugar. But you still get the flavor and creamy texture.

DELICIOUS DRESSING

Ingredients:

- 1 cup of filtered water
- 2 Tbs. ground flax seed
- ½ cup red wine vinegar
- 1 tsp. Dijon mustard
- 2 tsp. ground cumin
- 2 Tbs. grated fresh turmeric (or 2 tsp. dry)
- 2 garlic cloves, minced or finely chopped
- ½ tsp. black pepper (or 10 turns of a pepper mill to activate the turmeric)

So, I've replaced the oil with water and added 2 tablespoons of ground flax seed. This gives the dressing some flavour and texture. You can shake or whisk this dressing and put it in a jar to keep in the fridge.

I have eliminated the salt and sugar and haven't felt the need to replace them. If you need to sweeten it up, you could add a chopped date or a couple of raisins and blend in a blender until smooth.

If you need to add salt, add a stalk or two of celery instead. Celery contains enough sodium to get that salty taste. Or you can add some kelp powder. If you add a date or celery, you will have to use a blender to break them down. Then store in a jar in the fridge.

HUMMUS

Here's a compliant hummus recipe. I make this every couple of weeks. It is great when you can't be bothered to make a salad before dinner. A bunch of dipping vegetables and this hummus really takes the edge off your hunger and fills you up.

Ingredients:

- 1 ½ cups of chickpeas, either precooked or one small can, rinsed
- ¼ cup filtered water
- 1 Tbs. ground flax seed
- 1/3 cup fresh lemon juice
- 2 cloves garlic, lightly chopped
- 1 Tbs. red curry paste (I buy Thai Kitchen brand which comes in a small jar in the Asian food section of the supermarket.)

1. Put all the ingredients in a food processor, blender or Veggie Bullet. Blend until smooth. Use a tablespoon or two of water to thin it out if it is too thick.

2. Put it in a 2-cup glass container with a lid. The rest can go in a 1-cup container. This is the container you will serve the hummus into and wash daily. Use a clean spoon to serve from the main container to your daily container to stop contamination. This is so the hummus lasts longer without going off.

3. It easily lasts for a week or two. It will thicken up slightly as the days go by.

WHITE BEAN CHEEZ SAUCE

This is the sauce that you can put on your baked potatoes and steamed vegetables. It is absolutely delicious and will keep for about 2 weeks in the fridge.

At the beginning of this chapter, I said that on Friday you will soak the beans overnight. On Saturday you will cook the beans, then after they cool you can make this cheez sauce. This recipe is super simple. Only the beans are the time-consuming part. In a pinch you could use canned cannellini beans. But the sauce will not be as creamy as when you use small white navy beans.

Ingredients:

- 2 cups dry small white beans (navy beans) = 6 cups cooked
- 1 1/3 cups nutritional yeast
- 1½ cups filtered water
- 3 tsp. dry Italian herbs
- 1 tsp. onion powder
- 1 tsp. garlic powder

Blend until smooth. You can store in glass jars in the fridge. This also freezes well but don't freeze in jars, they tend to crack. Use one of your 4-cup glass storage containers.

WHOLE GRAINS AND STARCHY VEGETABLES

RICE

I prepare 2 cups dry rice every week. I easily manage to go through it too. Yum. Two cups dry yields about 6 cups cooked rice. I like brown long grain rice or the rice blends. But any rice that you like is fine. I have a rice cooker but only use it in emergencies as it only holds 1 cup of raw rice. If you are contemplating buying a rice cooker, go for the bigger one that will hold 2 or more cups of raw rice. Otherwise, here is my stovetop method for cooking rice.

1. Use a big enough pot to hold 6 cups of cooked rice.
2. Measure out 2 cups of rice into a small mesh strainer and rinse under cold water.
3. Follow the directions on the package for ratio of rice to water and the cooking time. (For example, the rice blend I use is a 1:1.5 ratio of rice to water and only takes 25 minutes).
4. For brown long grain rice, I use 2 cups of rinsed rice to 4 cups of filtered water.
5. Bring the pot up to boil, turn down the heat to low and cover immediately.
6. Let cook for 40-45 minutes. Try not to peek.
7. Remove from heat, fluff with a fork and let stand for 5 minutes with the lid on.
8. Remove the lid and let it cool completely. Once it is cooled you can transfer the rice into the 4-cup glass storage containers. You will keep one in the fridge and the other two you can freeze for later as needed.

QUINOA

Quinoa a super versatile grain and a good source of protein. It is super easy to cook as well. You use a similar method to cooking rice. I use 1 cup dry which also yields about 3 - 4 cups cooked.

1. Use a big enough pot to hold 4 cups of cooked quinoa.
2. Measure out 1 cup of quinoa into a small mesh strainer and rinse under cold water.
3. Put the rinsed quinoa in the pot with 2 cups of filtered water.
4. Bring the pot up to boil, turn down the heat to low and cover immediately.
5. Let cook for 20 minutes. Try not to peek.
6. 6. Remove from heat, fluff with a fork and let stand for 5 minutes with the lid on.
7. Remove the lid and let it cool completely. Once it is cooled you can transfer the quinoa into the 4-cup glass storage container and store in the fridge.
8. I have planned for you to make the Quinoa Tabouleh for Sunday. That's when you have your cutting board and citrus juicer hard at work but you could make it on the same day if you wish.

TABOULEH

This is the dish that I add to my breakfast salad which gives me some satiating starch.

Ingredients

- 3-4 cups cooked quinoa
- 1 small can chickpeas (garbanzo beans) or 2 cups cooked
- 1 medium tomato, jelly and seeds removed, finely diced
- ¼ medium red onion, finely diced
- 1 cup parsley, finely chopped
- 2 lemons, juiced

Combine all the ingredients in a large bowl with a lid and store in the fridge.

OATMEAL

Oatmeal is super versatile and easy to take with you to work. It is highly satiating and is great to have as a second breakfast after your salad to keep you full until lunch time. If you like a firmer oatmeal you can add chia seeds. The ratio of oats to water is 1:2. Here's a recipe that makes 1 medium serving.

Ingredients:

- ½ cup rolled oats
- 1 cup boiling purified water
- 1 cup mixed berries (frozen, thawed)
- 1 tsp. chia seeds (optional: for a firmer oatmeal)

Method:

1. Add oats to a jar or bowl. (and chia seeds if using)
2. Pour boiling water over the oats, cover and let sit for 5 minutes.
3. Add mixed berries to the top.
4. Stir to mix and enjoy.

Note: To thaw frozen fruit quickly, put the fruit in a bowl, fill the sink with hot water and sit the bowl in the hot water. This heats the bowl slowly and the fruit thaws in about 5 minutes.

Overnight Method:

1. Add oats (and chia seeds) to a jar.
2. In a measuring cup, add frozen berries then add water to the 1 cup line. Pour the water   and berries into the jar. If added separately, the oatmeal will be too runny.
3. Put on the lid and shake to mix.
4. Store in the fridge overnight and it will be ready to eat the next morning.

APPLE CRUMBLE

This is a delicious way to have your filling oats for your second breakfast. This recipe is SOFAS free (meaning it contains no salt, oil, flour, sugar, alcohol or salt). This is a health-promoting take on a super fattening comfort food on a cold winter day.

Ingredients

- 4 large Granny Smith apples, peeled, cored and sliced
- 2-4 sweet apples (apples with red on the skin are usually sweet), peeled, cored and sliced
- ½ cup organic unsweetened apple juice
- 2 cups organic rolled oats
- 1 cup unsweetened apple sauce
- 1 ½ tsp cinnamon

Method

1. Preheat oven to 350 degrees (400 if your oven doesn't get hot enough)
2. Core, peel and slice the apples and place in a deep casserole dish. Make sure you have one with a lid.
3. Pour apple juice over apples.
4. In a medium mixing bowl, add the oatmeal and cinnamon and stir to combine. Add the apple sauce and stir to combine until all the oatmeal is wet and the mixture resembles cookie dough.
5. Using a large spoon, spoon the mixture onto the apples and then smear to make an even coat over the apples.

6. Cover the casserole dish with the lid (or tin foil if you must) and put in the oven for 30 minutes.

7. After 30 minutes remove the lid. Bake for an extra 15 to 30 minutes until the oatmeal forms a nice crust and apples are cooked.

8. This makes 6-8 servings depending on how large a serving you want. Enjoy hot or cold.

BAKED POTATOES

Baked potatoes are super versatile and store all week long in the fridge. Delicious. I use the extra-large baking Russet potatoes and eat ½ of one cut lengthwise for my lunch.

So, I bake 4 of the extra-large potatoes or 8 medium potatoes every week. These are the directions for the extra-large potatoes. You can adapt the cooking time if you are using smaller potatoes.

Method

1. Preheat oven to 400 degrees.
2. Scrub the potatoes using a brush to remove any dirt. Check the potatoes for damage. You might have to cut out any black bits from harvesting damage.
3. Channel your Norman Bates and stab some holes in the potato. Three or 4 stabs for each potato should do it.
4. Place the potatoes directly on the middle rack of the oven and bake for about 1 ½ hours.
5. Once the timer is done. Turn off the oven and leave the potatoes in there. Later when they are cool enough to remove with your bare hands, leave them on the counter to cool completely.
6. Store in a large Ziploc bag in the fridge. They store well for a week in the bag. Every other day, I take out a potato and cut it lengthwise. I eat half with my cheez sauce and put the remaining half back in the bag with its buddies.

Legumes

Farts are internationally funny. When I was teaching English in Indonesia it was a guaranteed method to get the students talking and laughing by sharing their funniest or most embarrassing fart story. Around the world people have problems with gas and beans are not always to blame but often get the credit. I even used it as an excuse not to become a vegetarian when a friend was preaching the merits of a vegetarian diet. It's too bad she didn't know what I know now about the soaking and preparation of beans to make them more easily digestible.

To cut down on cooking time, you must soak your beans. Soaking is critical in increasing the digestibility of beans. Besides the electric company will send you a personalized thank you letter if you don't soak them. They'll take forever to boil.

An Instapot has made my life so much easier. It took me a year to get up the courage to use it. I always thought it would explode like in the old movies. But once I had mustered the courage to use it, I have never looked back. The soaked white navy beans I use in the cheez sauce only take 5 minutes to cook in a pressure cooker. In reality it takes longer as the machine has to get up to pressure first. But it is fast, hassle free, and safe.

But before we cook them, we have to soak them. Lots of people who are not accustomed to eating beans get terrible gas. If you don't take steps to strengthen your digestive system and prepare beans properly, get a dog to blame the gas on.

Soaking and Cooking Dried Beans

We need to soak beans because they are coated with phytic acid. This protects the bean from animals and bacteria. By soaking the beans with a little acid, you break down this coating. Then the beans are more easily digested. Also, the nutrients are more bioavailable for assimilation and absorption.

Canned beans are not soaked properly so the phytic acid is not broken down. This leads to gas and bloating. Beans that are properly prepared do NOT cause gas and bloating.

How to Prepare Dried Beans:

- Soak one-part beans with four parts of filtered water. Add a small amount of lemon juice or apple cider vinegar (ACV) to the water.
- Soak 12-24 hours. The longer the better to improve digestibility. Throw away the soak water and rinse the beans.
- Add the beans to a big pot with lots of water. Bring to a boil and skim off the foam. Think of every bubble as a potential fart that won't get the opportunity to ruin your day.
- Reduce heat and simmer, partially covered until beans are tender. Check occasionally and add more water if necessary.
- Fennel or cumin seeds may be added to cooking water for greater digestibility.
- As a general rule, beans double in bulk after cooking.
- Cooking times vary for different kinds of beans so it is best to cook them separately. The average cooking time for beans is 1 – 1½ hours.

Lentils cook pretty fast so I don't bother to soak them overnight. But if you tend to get gassy with lentils, soak them for a couple of hours in water with an acid before cooking.

In most soup recipes, you can add dry, rinsed lentils to the soup straight away and they cook in about ½ an hour. If you do decide to soak them, cut 10 minutes off the cooking time so that you do not overcook them.

Freezing Cooked Legumes

Beans and lentils freeze really well. Also, they tend to go off quickly once they are cooked so I always freeze them and use them as I go. After the beans are cooked, I drain off the water and rinse in a colander. Once they are cool, I put them into Ziploc freezer bags and try to freeze them flat.

When I need some beans for a recipe, I open the Ziplock and expose a part of the beans. I put a colander in the sink and rinse the exposed part under hot water. This way I can break off what I need and leave the rest frozen and intact. I can then return the remaining beans to the freezer.

THREE BEAN CHILI

This recipe makes 6 -7 2-cup servings.

Ingredients:

- a little filtered water for 'frying'
- 1 large onion, diced
- 3 bell peppers, diced
- 1 Tbs chili powder
- 1 Tbs cumin
- 1 Tbs oregano
- 1½ cups filtered water
- 1½ cups cooked kidney beans*
- 1½ cups cooked black beans*
- 1½ cups cooked pinto beans*
- 1 large can no-salt diced tomatoes
- pepper to taste

** If you don't have beans cooked you can use a small can of each type or a mixed bean medley. Make sure that you rinse the beans thoroughly before adding them to the chili.

Method:

1. Heat a pot with a little water over medium-low heat.
2. Sweat the onion until softened, about 5-10 minutes.
3. Add bell peppers, chili powder, and cumin. Stir and cook for another minute.
4. Add all the beans, canned diced tomatoes and water to onion mixture.
5. Bring the chili to a boil. Then simmer for 20 - 30

minutes to develop the flavors.

6. Let the chili cool completely and put into the 2-cup glass storage containers. You can freeze the extras but leave one in the fridge for Monday night.

7. Serve it over rice. You can add some salt-free salsa to add more heat.

GREEN LENTIL CURRY

This recipe makes 6-7 2-cup servings

Ingredients:

- 7 cups of filtered water
- 2 cups dry green lentils
- 2 bay leaves
- 1 medium onion, chopped
- 6 cloves garlic, finely chopped
- 1 Tbs. dry ginger
- 1 tsp turmeric powder
- 1 tsp curry powder
- ¼ cup cilantro leaves, chopped
- Juice of 1 lemon or lime
- Black pepper to taste, I use 10 turns of the pepper mill

Method:

1. Rinse lentils and set aside. If you have soaked them for a couple of hours this cuts down on the cooking time by 10 minutes.

2. In a large pot, add a little water for 'frying'. Add the

onions and cook for 15 minutes until golden brown. Add the garlic, bay leaves, ginger, turmeric, and curry. Stir in and add a little water to continue cooking for 1 minute.

3. Add the water and lentils into the big pot and stir together. Bring to a boil. Reduce and cover with a lid and continue to simmer for another 20 minutes. (30 minutes if you didn't presoak the lentils).
4. Add the cilantro leaves, lemon juice and black pepper and stir to incorporate.
5. Remove from the heat. Remove and discard the bay leaves. Let cool and put into 2-cup glass containers. You can freeze them for later use.
6. Serve this over rice or potatoes.

Our next chapter is about the scale. I am going to show you how to make the scale your friend instead of an enemy. How to make that scale reinforce your self esteem rather than tear you down and make you doubt yourself.

TASKS

1. Make sure that you have all the basic equipment available to you and ready to go. You should already have most of this stuff. If you don't, see if you can borrow some items from a friend. Don't worry about getting an Instapot if you don't have one. You can make do with using a big pot.
2. Make sure that you have all of your storage containers ready to go as well.
3. Plan for three days of cooking prior to your start day.

If you can do it in two you are a rock star. If you have lots of pots, you can double up on your tasks to make it more efficient. For example, I have two big pots so I can cook the Chili in one and the Lentil Curry in the other. This way, I am chopping and cooking the onions for both pots simultaneously.

Chapter Seven

Yo-Yo Dieting and The Scale

The first serious diet I went on was calorie counting. I was eighteen and wanted to look beautiful for my wedding. Over the course of 3 months, I lost 25 pounds on a super restrictive calorie reduced diet. It was not healthy and I managed to stay well under 1000 calories a day. I can still remember it like it was yesterday. I ate 2 boiled hot dogs on 2 pieces of bread each with 2 tablespoons of hotdog relish. That was lunch or dinner the other meal was chicken noodle soup from a dehydrated package. Apart from diet soda, coffee and sugar free gum this was all I would eat for 3 months. Not a vitamin or mineral to be found. That whole time not one person asked me where I was getting my protein, calcium, or Omega 3s from. I must say that I looked fabulous when I tried on and the dress. Here I was three weeks out from my wedding, looking better than ever and life was good.

The problem was I had these three weeks before the wedding. What was I going to eat? I couldn't possibly bare going back to calorie counting. And then there were all the parties and entertaining and food and guests staying in town before the big day. What about my showers with cake and tea?

What about the hen party with booze and salty snacks?

I tried to keep myself somewhat under control. But when we got the dress back from the seamstress all ready for the big day, I must have put on 5 to 8 pounds. The dress was snug to say the least. I had to buy a girdle and quick so I would be able to do up the long zipper. Well, the wedding went off fine. The zipper didn't break through the ceremony, the pictures, the dinner, and the toasts. I was uncomfortable but it looked like I would make it!

We had the first dance and second dance. Still good. But on the third dance a guest stepped on my train by accident and I came spilling out of the entire back of my dress. The zipper had just given up the ghost right there on the dance floor. I can't blame the zipper or the seamstress. But my new husband and I had to high tail it out of the reception. We went home and changed and then returned for more dancing. At least it gave the older and sober crowd an opportunity to leave the wedding at a reasonable hour. Few people knew what had actually happened but you can bet it is burned in my memory. I still have the dress but I was never able to fit into it again.

A True Yo-Yo Dieter

Let's say you wake up one morning and get on the scale and your magic number is there. You rub your eyes in disbelief and step off and stand back on the scale. You have done it! It's time to celebrate! You have been thinking about this day for months. How will you celebrate?

Well, if you have a history of yo-yo dieting, there is no

better way to celebrate than with food. All the food you have been restricting from your diet for the last 3 to 6 months. Diet programs always warn you about a maintenance plan after you reach your goal weight. But they rarely go into great detail because they know that their diet is unsustainable in the long run.

So inevitably after all that hard work and deprivation you have to reward yourself. And you have done nothing but think about food for the last three months. So naturally your reward is going to be some forbidden food.

But one meal leads to the next and always tastes like more. That maintenance program still seems awfully restrictive. And you are back to eating the way you did before. No wonder the weight comes back on.

When the South Beach Diet came out, I had to try it. At first it was great. I lost a lot of weight the first two weeks. This was phase 1 the most restrictive phase. But then when I went to phase 2, I didn't lose as much so I was getting disheartened. So, I started again with phase 1 but I didn't lose any weight. What the….? So, what's with this? I don't lose weight on phase 2 and I don't lose weight on phase 1 again. What can I do? I gave up and waited for the next diet sensation.

After years of yo-yo dieting, I couldn't keep on the diet programs for any significant length of time. I had spiraled down to a week-long cycle. The scale became a measurement of my self worth. If I weighed myself once a week, this was my standard pattern. I would start whatever diet on a Monday and be an A+ student until Saturday when I would step on the scale just to check. I didn't wait until Sunday and here is why.

If my weight went down, I would want to celebrate with food. It was Saturday, I had a day to take off the weight I put on from a pig out and after all, I would be back on my diet on Monday. I would tell myself that I deserved a reward.

I would celebrate but somehow one off-plan meal became an off-plan day. Then two days. And then it was almost impossible to start again on Monday. I was readdicted to salt, sugar and fat. I would have to wait until the beginning of next month to start again. You know, start with a clean slate. But wait. The beginning of next month is on a Thursday that won't work. I should start on the Monday. So, let's make it the first Monday of next month. I spent years doing this.

But if the news was bad when I stepped on the scale on Saturday morning. I mean I only lost a pound. Or nothing. Or gained! And I had worked so hard. Well, the diet didn't work did it. It's easier to go off the rails if the diet didn't work. I had the perfect excuse to binge eat until I couldn't bear my self loathing any longer and try something new.

I didn't understand the truth about what I was weighing, I would assume it was fat I was measuring and not water. I would even check and recheck the dial for the calibrator of the scale to make sure that it was EXACTLY on zero and hadn't shifted.

Don't be a Scale Monkey

Are you the kind of person who jumps on and off the scale hoping that by some miracle the number will change? Have a bowel movement better check the scale. Had a great pee better check the scale. Dehydrated from a long walk in the sun or worse yet from partying all night…better check the scale. Unfortunately, the number is never much better than what you had anticipated. In some instances, it either hasn't moved or has in fact gone up a pound.

Well, that was me for years. My mood could instantly be changed based on what was on the scale. Somehow in my mind I had convinced myself that the weight would come off faster than I had packed it on. Afterall, that's what the big diet companies are selling. If you weigh in too often you will always be disappointed. You can never see that big number over a few days. That is not how our bodies work.

According to Dr. Doug Lisle women typically gain 10 pounds of fat for every decade they live. This weight gain comes on in dribs and drabs because of the Standard American Diet. That comes down to a few extra calories every day over the mark. Only a few extra calories more than your body needs and that you are not burning off leads to fat storage.

This doesn't even include the massive amount of weight you can gain and lose as a yo-yo dieter. Popular diet programs make big promises and can deliver in the short term. You can lose X amount of weight in X number of days doing it the X way! This is the formula that we have bought into again and again and it is true in the short term. You can lose weight quickly while depriving yourself and exercising like a fiend.

But you WILL put that weight back on and then some if you do not sustain the diet. And fad diets are unsustainable. You cannot continue weighing your food and calculating calories until the end of your days. What a waste of life and time. Using calorie density is a much easier and sustainable way.

What they don't like to tell you is that you have to consider what you are weighing. Initially everyone is going to lose water weight, or glycogen stores with exercise. That's what big diet companies are counting on. Everyone can lose weight at first. But what is this weight comprised of?

What are You Weighing?

So, what are we really weighing when we step of the scale? Well, there is your skeleton and the density of your bones. There are your internal organs, muscles, and tendons. There is body fat enough to protect your organs and give you some reserves in the event of famine. There is water and our bodies have plenty of it. Men are 60% water and women are 50% water. There is feces and urine waiting for their opportunity to leave the body. There is glycogen in the muscles and liver stored so that we can run away in the event of an attack. And, in the case of everyone reading this book, there is extra body fat.

So, if you weigh yourself every day there will only be three factors that will change on a daily basis. But it won't be body fat. It will be water in the form of urine and perspiration, feces, and stored glycogen from your liver and muscles.

Now, will your tight jeans fit better if you lose a pound of waste in a day? No, they won't. Yet we have bought into the marketing ploys of the big diet companies. We think that we should be able to drop huge amounts of fat in a short period of time using their special plan.

Even fans of the TV show the Biggest Loser will see

phenomenal numbers lost at the first weigh in. This is usually followed by disappointing numbers in the second week. Well, you ask, how can they do that? I mean, lose all that weight in the first week. It is simple, salt.

Before they arrive on the ranch, they are eating a highly-processed diet. And they are eating huge quantities of unhealthy foods. These foods contain the killer triad of salt, sugar and oil. The contestants are taken off these three substances for a week. The salt is cut out entirely. All that water that is needed by the body to dilute the sodium isn't necessary anymore. As a result, the body sheds a huge amount of water. Not fat but water. That's what they are losing.

Inevitably later in the season the women would have some sort of unexplained weight gain or no weight loss at all for a week. I realize now that this could be due to water retention related to their period. So, in effect, their poor results are based on water weight loss rather than true fat loss. That's no way to live.

The Solution

So how do we handle this phenomenon. How do we know we are losing fat not water? How do we break this cycle that our success is based on an arbitrary and inaccurate number on the scale? The answer is simple and also motivating. We only weigh in once a month. We weigh in and take our measurements for 3 consecutive days and take the average.

This way we have an accurate reading of our actual weight loss. For women, the expected result is 2 pounds of fat per month. You say hey wait a minute, only two pounds? That doesn't sound very impressive. Well, it is if you understand what two pounds of fat loss represents in a three-dimensional image. That is two personal-sized water bottles. Now that you can visualize it, that is a lot of fat.

Imagine the biological processes that need to take place on a cellular level. To lose those two pounds of fat a month, your liver can't be overworked. The liver has a lot of jobs and is not designed to process so many extra toxins every day.

Big Fat Loss is a Big Bodily Process

Is your current diet and lifestyle toxic? Are there lots of additives and preservatives in your foods? Meat is full of pesticides. The pesticides are incorporated into the flesh of animals. This is because the feed grain is sprayed with pesticides. Non-organic fruits and vegetables are also sprayed with pesticides. But there is no bigger contributor of toxins than highly processed foods. Highly-processed foods contain lots of fat, sugar and salt. They also contain preservatives, food dyes, additives, flavor enhancers and stabilizers. The body doesn't recognize these things as food because they are not really food. So, to protect itself the body must either expel it quickly or safely store it.

The body needs to protect itself from this onslaught of toxins. So, to not overburden the liver, the body stores the toxins inside the fat cells. This protects the body. The fat cell surrounds the toxins like a bubble pack will protect a fragile package.

When you clean up your diet, the overburdened liver can catch up on its work and begin cleaning up the inside of the body. All the new healthy foods contain lots of vitamins and minerals. All these nutrients support the cells of the cleansing organs. This support helps to regenerate and refresh them. Then the organs can rid the body of the toxins stored in the fat cells.

That is why detox diets are so popular now. We understand that the body needs a rest from toxins. This means eating a clean diet long enough to allow the body a chance to catch up on getting rid of toxins. It is also why you feel so icky especially if you have had a diet high in chemicals. You feel tired, with flu-like symptoms for the first 2 or 3 days. It is like last call at the bar. The organs are in a hurry to get the toxins out the door so that they can go about the job of cleaning up.

Your cleansing organs can finally catch up on all the cleansing and filtering. Then they can start with a clean slate and take on the task of disposing of the stored toxins in the fat cells.

People don't realize that they are alive on a cellular level. Every cell is alive and has a job to do. We feed our living cells dead food or food that isn't really food. Just a chemical concoction created in a lab and not in nature. Then we expect our bodies to do our bidding of processing it, which it tries to do but eventually the body can't keep up and we get a serious disease.

People are surprised when their bodies don't perform optimally. But they don't make the connection between non-foods and health. They think that their intellect can solve the problems with the body. They forget about the innate ability of the entire body to regenerate and heal itself. It's arrogance. You can't reason with a wild animal. You can not reason away your aches and pains or diseases. You have to give your cells, organs, and entire body what it was designed to eat to restore your health. This comes from eating whole plant-based foods that are nutrient rich.

Once you have started eating whole plant-based foods, your body is cleansing. Your liver has caught up with the day-to-day mess you have put your body in. It has been able to heal itself. Then, it is ready to dispose of those little packages of toxins stored in your fat cells.

Now that your body is not taking in fat through diet, all these extra fat cells can be utilized for energy. My ass had enough stored energy in it to light up a small city at one point I am sure of it. So, like a processing plant, the contents of the fat cell are broken down. The fat is utilized for energy. The toxins are safely removed from the body through elimination.

Our bodies are a miracle. They can take so much abuse and still bounce back to not only survive but thrive. And yet we are so impatient with this miracle. This process. It's like we are a horrible boss. We just stand there and tap our toe and say 'work faster, work faster, work faster'. We do not understand the complexity and time it takes to perform the tasks asked of the team.

When you eat a whole food plant-based diet every day, you will lose weight. You will be able to keep it off because this is your new way of eating. You are eating to treasure your body and take care of it. Then it can take care of you by providing a strong fit vessel to carry you through to the end of your days.

You can live without the fear of debilitating disease. Diseases caused by abusing your body with a modern diet we were not designed to consume. There is no *real* plateau when you eat this way. Your body will decide for you when you have achieved your ideal weight for your frame. It will reward you with optimal performance for the tasks it must perform.

A plateau in weight can be caused by many things. There will be times when your system will need to do some extra housekeeping that you are not always aware of. For example, fighting off a virus, or fighting off bacteria which can cause infection. Or fighting off ubiquitous chemicals in the air or water to keep your cells healthy. Do the work. The extra fat will come off.

There is no point in starting a calorie restrictive diet and gritting your teeth for 3 months. That kind of diet is unsustainable. You will only pack it all back on plus 10 pounds in time for Christmas dinner all in the same year. It is better knowing that you will be losing at least two pounds of fat a month for the next 12 months which equals 24 pounds! I don't know about you but EVERYONE who needs to lose weight looks better after losing 24 pounds.

Even if you have 100 pounds to lose, you will look and feel healthier and your self-confidence will be strong. You will know that every day you have put your health first and have worked hard to achieve this goal. You won't need people to tell you how good you look which of course you will. That's an added bonus. But your internal audience will be giving you a big thumbs up. You will be getting an A and sometimes an A+ every day for hitting your targets.

You won't be white knuckling it for the rest of your life making food or the scale the center of your universe. You are no longer thinking about what you can or cannot eat. You will have achieved great things with a sustainable plant-based whole foods diet. You will be off the roller coaster. You have your life back and you can live it with great joy knowing that you have conquered the monster.

There is something else that is a huge benefit for losing weight slowly and steadily. It's a big problem that the transformational quick weight loss programs do not like to talk about. It is loose skin and hair loss. If you lose the weight too quickly, the skin doesn't have the chance to bounce back especially if you are over 40. If you lose the weight gradually, your body has a chance to adjust accordingly and you won't have loose skin. If you are over 50, the chances that your skin will bounce back are declining. This is because we make less collagen as we age. That's another good reason to get started when you are younger.

Hair loss is also an issue with rapid weight loss. It is an indication that you are either ill or nutritionally starving. I have lost a lot of hair over the years from all the yo-yo dieting. Now my hair is holding fast again! I know it's because every day I flood my body with nutrients and keep out the toxins.

Rapid weight loss programs are more concerned about the number of calories rather than the nutrients in the foods. If the diet is made up of highly processed foods, the nutrients are lost in processing. As a result, your body is under stress because it thinks it is starving. The limited nutrients are used to repair and maintain the most important organs and processes. So, your hair is like the last dog to the bowl. Hair is not required for you to survive so the nutrients are diverted to the more important task of keeping you alive.

Using this plan, your body is not under stress because it knows it is not starving. It gets at least 4 pounds of food every day. And not just any food. It gets the most nutrient dense and least calorically dense foods. Only the very best foods to repair your body and return it to perfect equilibrium. These foods are the wide varieties of vegetables, fruit, whole grains and legumes. So, you will lose the extra fat, but you won't lose your hair.

The next chapter will help give you some peace. It will help you understand why you slip and what to do to avoid it. You will understand that it is not your fault but it is your responsibility. I discuss food addictions and food triggers. I also go into detail about night eating which is called cramming.

TASKS:

1. There is only one task. That's to weigh and measure yourself once a month for 3 consecutive days. ONCE A MONTH. If you have to, take the scale out of the bathroom. Put it away somewhere so you won't be tempted to check your weight early. If you are a scale monkey like me, it is the only way to break that cycle. Weighing yourself once a month really works, too. It is like waiting for Christmas. You know that the number on the scale for a month is as close to real as you can get. It will keep you compliant to your new way of eating too. You won't

want to eat off plan and sabotage the opportunity of seeing a real and rewarding loss on the scale.

Chapter Eight

What to Do If You Slip

Emotional Eating

Here is the truth about emotional eating. It is a cop out for when you purposefully go on a binge. You blame your day, stress level, significant other, or job. You are bored or lonely. There are tons of reasons to justify a binge. It's an excuse to eat comfort foods. What are comfort foods? Foods loaded with salt, sugar and fat. Mac and cheese, pizza, chocolate. It really is cold comfort because after the binge you do NOT feel comforted.

Why don't thin people all over the world suffer from emotional eating? Is it because they have no problems or stress? Is it because these billions of people never had a bad childhood or were never bullied? Were they never stressed, lonely or tired? Of course not.

The truth is that emotional eating can be triggered in our minds by any emotion. Happy? Want to celebrate? Sad, stressed, lonely, or tired? If you have food addictions you can find any reason that you need to justify your eating. Does your overweight cat or dog suffer from emotional eating? No. When your dog is begging under the dinner table, is he telling you with his eyes about what a rough day he has had? No. He is addicted to the fat, salt, and sugar just like you. But he can not justify it, the way you can.

Your addiction is tricking you into thinking it's a good idea to comfort yourself with food. Like any addict who falls off the wagon. If they have a particularly rough day, they can justify using. By partaking in their addictive substance, they will find great comfort in it. Saying to themselves that they aren't ready to deal with the day-to-day stress and need their crutch. Alcoholics do it. Cigarette smokers do it. People doing drugs do it as well.

It's tough for them but actually it is worse for you. This is because fattening foods are everywhere. And they are legal. You can be triggered by seeing an ad on tv, walking through a grocery store or smelling it in a restaurant. Popcorn in a movie theatre is bad for people like me who love popcorn. You can see, smell and hear it crunching all around you.

So, if it is not your emotions dictating what you are eating, it has to be a food addiction. From laboratory to factory to advertising to the shelves of your supermarket. Processed foods are very carefully engineered. They are designed to trigger those dopamine 'feel good' circuits in your brain. Companies spend millions of dollars to get you hooked on their products. They use a precise balance of fat, salt, and sugar. Stabilizers and other additives give these 'foods' a ridiculously long shelf life. And your addiction to them keeps you buying and eating more and more.

Do you really think the Party Pack of chips is for a party? The companies know that you are not buying it for a party. So does the cashier at your supermarket when they see you coming. The same goes for jumbo-sized chocolate bars. Those didn't exist when I was a kid. There was one size. The chocolate producers know you are not going to have the self control to eat one square a day. They are betting that you can't. They are banking on the addictive quality of their product to keep you coming back.

So how do alcoholics, smokers, and drug addicts solve their problem? They abstain from the thing that they are addicted to. For food it is difficult because as I said it is everywhere and legal and also a part of social and family life. We also need food to survive. This is why I spent a great deal of time on the chapter of having a clean environment. If your environment is clean, you can't help but stay on the right course.

When I was first starting this journey, I had everything in place. I had my kitchen cleaned out except for my skinny husband's off-plan foods. I had my bulk cooking done. Everything was ready and I could more or less survive for a week except for the odd clamshell of greens. Then my husband had a medical emergency and was taken to the hospital by ambulance. This was during COVID 19 so I had no way of going with him or contacting him once he was there. (A few days later I put his cell phone in a baggy and delivered it to the entrance of the hospital.) I called my wonderful and only sister who came up to stay with me for the whole time that he was in the hospital.

They had to keep my husband in the hospital for a week. A lot of tests had to be done to determine the next course of action. I couldn't go anywhere. I didn't want to miss the phone calls from the excellent nurses and doctors about my husband's health. I was obviously highly emotional. But because my environment was clean, I abstained from all 'comfort foods' and stayed on plan.

My sister, being the good sport that she is, ate my husband's off plan foods. And, at the end of the week, took the ice cream and non-healthy foods with her to feed her family. Even though I felt guilty about sending her home with this unhealthy food, I knew two things. If it stayed in the house either my husband or I would eat it. And I knew if she didn't already have this food, they would be buying it shortly on the next supermarket visit.

So, what do you do instead of emotional eating? Firstly, realize what this is. It is an excuse to give in to your food addictions. You've got a clean kitchen full of compliant food. If you are having a hard day for any reason, ask yourself what a person at goal weight would be doing.

For me there are a few choices. Sleep if you are overtired. Get out and exercise if you are stressed out. Or do some busywork like household chores if your mind is racing and you need to think something through.

Don't do things that trigger you to embrace your old eating behavior. For example, I love gangster movies. And if I watch the Godfather or Goodfellas, I want to eat big heaping plates of pasta. So, no more old gangster movies for me but I am okay with that because I know how they end.

Try to avoid watching TV. Instead watch supportive videos and presentations about the plant-based lifestyle. It will help affirm your choices by seeing others who are on the same journey and have achieved success. If you do slip, return to your new way of eating the very next meal. Don't beat yourself up about. You made a mistake. Move on and make this month count. In a 30-day month you will eat 90 meals. If you messed up once, that's still a huge improvement over your old way of eating. Get right back on the horse.

Cramming versus Binge Eating

Cramming happens at night after your compliant meal when you eat extra food. It is not unhealthy food but you feel compelled to cram in as much as you can before going to bed. Binge eating can start any time of day. These are addiction driven foods. You eat and eat and eat all the addictive foods you can consume. For example, you can cram carrots. You can cram plain baked potatoes. But you would never binge on plain baked potatoes. But a person could be addicted to the butter, the sour cream, the cheese or other fatty toppings that are put on top of them.

Cramming

You may wonder what cramming is and I take the word from Dr. Doug Lisle's explanation of the cramming circuit. This goes back to your ancestral brain for survival. Imagine you have eaten a compliant meal and you are satisfied but not totally full. There is no non-compliant food in the house but you just feel you need something more. This is when you start sniffing around the kitchen for the most calorie dense food you can find. You eat until you cannot eat any more. You find those raisins or your family member's stash of nuts. It is calorie dense and not on your plan and you eat that little bit more. Why? Why do you do this?

Dr. Doug Lisle is an evolutionary psychologist. He says that you do this because your ancestral brain is telling you to. It is telling you to get in as many calories as possible for survival.

Think about what it was like back in the day when it was feast or famine. People knew that they had to put on fat to get them through the times when there was very little or no food. So, when there was plenty of food, they would cram in as many calories as they could. This was to survive those lean times and live off their fat.

We don't have that problem anymore. The kitchen is always stocked and food is available everywhere. There is no reason to cram because your next meal is coming. You need to override this ancient brain impulse. Realize that your next meal is waiting for you in the fridge. You will not starve to death by morning.

There are three simple steps to perform to override the cram circuit. Have plenty of satisfying and filling starches for dinner. Put any leftovers away and wash your dishes. Then the kitchen is closed for the night.

Trigger Foods

These foods are the ones that are individual to you. They are the foods that if you eat just one it is never enough. You are addicted to them. You can not take or leave these foods. If you start with one it always leads to more and then you say to yourself, 'you know what would go good with this....' And you are off to the races on a true binge.

You may decide you deserve a reward for all your hard work. Or someone might serve it up for you as a special treat. Don't touch it. It is a trigger food which you can never get enough of. If you indulge in one of your trigger foods in a clean environment, you will never be able to leave it alone until it is all gone. This can lead to days and days of eating non-compliant food.

For example, my problem is with popcorn. I would buy my organic non-GMO popcorn and pop it in coconut oil with lots of salt and pepper. Amazing! I would pop, and pop and sometimes eat two huge bowls in a sitting. As the popcorn kernels disappeared, I would feel compelled to buy more to replace them. Afterall, there aren't enough kernels left to have even half a bowl of popcorn. Hardly worth the effort. Instead of throwing the remaining few kernels away, I would buy another package. And the vicious cycle would continue.

Trigger foods are hyper-palatable foods. This basically means they are super delicious and have been engineered to be so. They have all the components needed to rock the pleasure-seeking centers in your brain. They always contain either sugar, fat or salt or a combination of all three.

To combat your food triggers, you have to know thyself. Ask yourself what 5 foods would you take to a deserted island. What would they be? Or even one food? Whatever you answer it will be a food trigger. Imagine you are really hungry and at a giant buffet. You are going to choose the most hyper-palatable, calorie dense food you can find.

This is the easiest one. How do you keep sober around trigger foods? Well, you simply do not keep them in the house. If someone gives you a gift of chocolates, you regift it straight away. Or take the offending foods to work with you and let your co-workers enjoy it. Leftover candy or whatever, they will make short work of it. Keep it as far away from you as you can manage and always have nourishing healthy food ready to eat.

Be prepared and have a snack or meal with you. Don't ever be so unprepared and let yourself get so hungry that a trigger food will lure you into even tasting it.

When I first started eating this way, I started taking my giant salad to work with me. But I had the type of job that had a flexible finishing time. I would finish well before noon on most days. There were no breaks and the faster you worked, the sooner you could go home. As a result, I stopped taking my giant salad to work. It took too long to eat.

Some days were longer than others and I found I was unprepared and getting hungry. I knew I had at least an hour or two to go before I would be free to get home to a compliant feast.

In these instances, I always had spirulina tablets in my bag. Spirulina is a type of algae. Drinking it powdered is gross but in a tablet form you can pop it like any pill. It is a super green and has the benefit of balancing blood sugar. So, your hunger will go away until you have an opportunity to eat. I always carry spirulina in my bag just in case I can't get to compliant food in time. You can read more about the benefits of spirulina in Chapter 10.

The next chapter deals with common challenges that you will face during your weight loss journey. You will learn how to deal with difficult people. Forewarned is forearmed.

Chapter Nine

How to Deal With the Haters

I can still remember the first Christmas I had when I turned vegan. I had about seven months behind me and we were going to my in-law's house for Christmas dinner. My sister-in-law knew I was vegan as I had called her before to discuss that I would be bringing my own food to the meal. I came prepared with my own turkey-like seitan and potatoes and vegan gravy. I also brought a big tray of vegetables with three kinds of hummus for everyone to enjoy. This wasn't a big sit-down affair as there were too many people to sit at one table. So, you could serve yourself and eat where you want.

We started with the appetizers that everyone had brought. I set out my big tray of vegetables and hummus. Before anyone had a chance to dig in, my sister-in-law announced, 'That's vegan.' Now I don't know if it was the way she said it. But for most of the people she could have said, 'that's radioactive'. Because hardly any people tried it and the brave ones who did had tons of questions about why it was vegan.

I had the typical question of 'where do you get your protein?' Thankfully, I was well versed on this question. But the discussion got to feel combative and argumentative. I could have said that I was pro-Trump when no one else at the party was.

After the grilling, and debating I was exhausted and a little downcast. I couldn't come up with enough scientifically-backed responses to sway the crowd. Now, when I go there, I am accepted for my lifestyle choices. But that is because of my tenacity of continuing my vegan lifestyle.

I am no longer concerned if anyone tries or doesn't try my offerings. When I go to a family gathering, I put the food out like everyone else and keep my mouth shut about it. It's food after all. And it is always the most nutritious option for everyone. Not to mention delicious.

Dealing with Difficult People

The conundrum of how to deal with difficult people can go a few ways. First, there are the people who become almost combative. They feel that their poor dietary choices are being attacked and as a result their esteem within the group is being attacked. They want to know where you get your protein/calcium/Omega 3s from. They are determined to debate you.

Then there are the supposedly well-meaning saboteurs. These are the ones that say guilt ridden sentences such as, 'But I made your favorite especially for you'. They knew beforehand that you had started a new way of eating for your health. Yet they are trying to guilt you into eating the treat. They too are trying to protect their lifestyle choices and their own standing with the group.

Then there are the people that are ignorant about nutrition.

They will ask the same questions as the combative ones. But they are more curious and are interested in being informed. This ironically is the most tiresome group. They will expect you to talk about nutrition all night long instead of talking about other interesting topics. It's like teaching a class on nutrition for 4-6 hours. It is exhausting.

So how do you deal with these three types of people? You want to give yourself the opportunity to pass a pleasant evening with your friends. I am on various vegan, health and weight loss Facebook groups. These groups have a myriad of opinions about how to deal with these people. Some of the responses are either downright rude or they are attacking the other person's esteem. This is never fun at a party and neither side wants to come off looking like an asshole.

Dr. Doug Lisle presented the best alternative to this question. He has solved this problem in the easiest and least combative way.

Simply say that you are conducting an experiment. That you have had some health challenges in the past. And the doctor would like you to try this new way of eating to see if it helps. Then you can add that you have been eating this way for a while. You feel much better. And that you think you are going to continue eating this way to see if it helps to improve your health. That's all you have to say.

Throw your doctor under the bus if you have to. After all, you have already told him of your intentions before you started this journey so it's not a lie. When I heard this explanation, I felt relieved. There isn't a good enough comeback to debate with if the doctor isn't at the party. People respect doctors.

Ironically, at the same Christmas dinner, one person had some serious health problems. His doctor determined that he had celiac disease which means no gluten. Nobody said anything about it. Afterall it was under the doctor's guidance that he should never eat gluten. The argument was a non-starter.

After you have addressed this issue with the questioner, move on to talk about other things. That is the reason you are at the gathering to begin with. It's to catch up with and talk about what the other people are doing.

There is a great way of passing the time at a big party that doesn't involved food or drink. Besides talking to relatives or friends, if you are not a big talker, take pictures. It helps pass the time in a healthy way and most people enjoy having a record of the gathering.

Meals Out

I do not recommend eating out as it is impossible to control what does or doesn't go into your meal. You can tell the waiter no added salt, sugar or oil. But in some cases, like with rice or potatoes, salt and oil are added during the bulk cooking process. Or the message just doesn't reach the chef. The preparation of the meal is out of your control so assume the worst and try to eat at home as many meals as you can.

It is also difficult if you are eating with people who don't know you are on a special diet. It can make everyone uncomfortable. Especially if you a studying the menu and questioning the waiter for a long period of time. I know that I have made dear friends and loved ones uncomfortable with their own menu choices. And as a result, have put their esteem at stake. Don't make other people uncomfortable. If you have to explain, just give them the doctor's orders speech and everything will be fine.

If you are dining out for a special occasion you can plan for it. There are some things that you can do beforehand. You want to ensure the cleanest most compliant meal possible.

Research the menus online before you select a restaurant. This cuts down on so much trouble and disappointment before the meal starts.

My family likes to celebrate Father's Day at a restaurant. A few years ago, someone chose a new venue and it was a banquet style meal to celebrate the day. What I didn't know was that it must have been called a carnivore's delight banquet. Because even the vegetable dishes had either meat or dairy or both in them. There was only some lettuce leaves and a few garnish vegetables for me to pick through. They were not serving anything other than the buffet that day. It was uncomfortable for everyone. I felt sorry for the family member who had chosen this venue. Everyone assumed that there would be plenty of at least vegetarian options. But this was not the case.

The next time we met for Father's Day, I got the name of the restaurant beforehand. It also had a buffet style layout for Father's Day. I was able to research their menu online and found that they had lots of options for me so I could relax and enjoy the day.

There are times you can't prepare. You are going in cold to

a new restaurant or banquet situation. You can't research the menu beforehand. Eat before you leave home but leave a little room in case you want to try something. Remember you are not really there for the food. You are there to share stories and connect with the people at the table.

You can also call the restaurant well before to ask questions about how the food is prepared. Find out if they can be prepared without oil, salt or sugar.

My husband and I have a Greek restaurant that is very special to us. It was where we went for our wedding luncheon after the ceremony. Being a Greek restaurant, it was hard to find a vegan option. I called the restaurant and found that the chef was delighted to make a vegan meal especially for me. I had beautifully grilled vegetables with rice and a modified Greek salad.

Since our wedding, this is our place to go to celebrate our anniversary. Prior to the day, I always call and review my meal options and specify no oil or salt. They are always accommodating and I can rest easy knowing that what I am eating is prepared the way I need it to be.

Making your gathering not about the food at all would be even better. A picnic with compliant foods, meeting at a park or beach, meeting in a coffee house for herbal tea and a chat. Going to a local sporting event gives you plenty of time to chat. Or for a walk in the forest. If you are more adventurous and you are fit enough for it and want to mark a special day, try zip-lining or kayaking. My point is that it doesn't have to be about food.

Non-Compliant Household Members

If you live alone, your kitchen and fridge are your own. Once it is cleaned out and restocked you never have to worry about other people's non-compliant food. But, most people have at least one other person in the house that they have to think about. How do you deal with these people?

When my husband and I were dating I was eating meat. I became a vegan just after we got married. That was more of a change than this new way of eating was. Frankly, apart from the weight loss, I don't think he has even noticed. So, if you are already eating a plant-based diet the transition will not seem as drastic to them.

You will want to talk to your partner about the changes that you are making. Especially before you start clearing out the kitchen. You will tell them that the doctor thinks you should conduct an experiment. Your doctor wants you to give up salt, sugar, and fat to improve your health. Tell them that you need their support to make these changes.

It could go two ways. The best-case scenario is that they are all for it and will join in with you. But if they are food addicted you will have some problems and there will definitely be some kickback.

Develop a live-and-let-live attitude towards the other people in the house. Let them make their own choices. Do not preach or push your new way of eating on your partner. Let your own increased health, vitality and weight loss speak for you.

But also stand your ground, don't cave in to pressure. There shouldn't be any if your partner really loves you and wants to support you. Imagine that you came home from the doctor with a cancer diagnosis. The doctor gave specific orders of what you needed to avoid. There would be all kinds of support from your family.

Think of it like this. To accommodate everyone there will be compromises on both sides that will have to be made. If possible, get them to eat their non-compliant food out of your house. Or, like I did with my husband, I don't prepare his food anymore. I don't want to be cooking meat and he was an excellent cook and preferred his own cooking anyway.

I sometimes refer to my husband as a lazy vegan. If he didn't feel like cooking, he would end up eating and enjoying what I had prepared. But, when cooking every day got to be too much for him, I ordered him Meals-on-Wheels and the problem was taken care of. Some people prepare their compliant food and have their partners cook their own meat. Then their partner can eat the compliant food as a side dish. It's easy enough to do.

Another thing that you can do is don't shop for them. Buy only compliant foods if possible. You don't send an alcoholic to the liquor store. So, don't find yourself buying junk food for your family. Because if it is in the house you will eat it. I have made my husband a special box that has his snacky kinds of foods in there like granola bars and roasted nuts. These foods are not food triggers for me so I don't have a problem buying them or having them in the house.

But, if I put cheezies and corn chips in that box, I would be nose deep in the box the same day I bought them. So, know your triggers and keep them out of the house. If you don't feel strong enough to do this, consider buying a food safe. Or you can put a lock on one of the cupboards or have a second fridge/freezer for the non-compliant food. There is always a way to solve your individual challenges in this area. Put yourself first for once and make these changes.

In the next chapter, I will answer some common questions that come up along your journey. I cover topics such as the importance of regular exercise and how to keep motivated.

Chapter Ten

Common Questions Answered

What are Compliant Foods?

First you might notice that I mention compliant foods and compliant cooking quite a bit. This means that you are eating whole foods that are plant-based and low in calorie density. They include vegetables, fruit, whole grains and legumes. Compliant also means that you are not using any salt, oil or sugar in your food. Chef AJ goes a step farther. She calls her program SOFAS free. Or get off your SOFAS. This means no salt, oil, flour, alcohol or sugar are added to her recipes.

What About Exercise?

Okay, it is time to talk about exercise. You may ask is exercise part of my daily targets? That is up to you. Exercise is not necessary to burn fat if you are following a low-calorie density diet. But as your self esteem increases and your health improves you will want to move your body. Find activities that you love to do. Think about sports you enjoyed when you were a kid. Perhaps you can reintroduce one of these to your repertoire.

If you love the gym, by all means join but make sure it is because you love going there. If you don't love the gym you can definitely skip it. It doesn't have to be a target unless you decide to make it one. So, if you don't want to go to the gym you can find other ways to move your body. Find an activity that builds your self esteem rather than deflates it.

Yoga and meditation are great things you can do at home. You can search for programs that interest you on your computer. Even on TV there are channels that have yoga programs. Yoga is wonderful for developing balance and flexibility.

Walking the dog. It's good for you and your pet will appreciate it. Walking is the cheapest and easiest exercise for when you are starting out. Have you seen the film Fat, Sick and Nearly Dead 2? In the film, the cardiologist tells Joe Cross that ½ an hour of walking every day will stop heart disease. And 1 hour a day will reverse the damage. That's great news. As you get fitter, you can work up to that or divide your walks into 2 or 3 manageable times during the day.

You can work with weights or use your own body weight. Exercises like calisthenics, yoga and Pilates are a great way to keep your muscles strong. Working with weight will help to maintain and, in some cases, increase muscle mass. Muscle health is critical in keeping your metabolism high and increasing muscle tone.

There is a trick with exercise. According to Dr. Doug Lisle, exercise makes it easier to keep your willpower strong. Especially if you start the day with some exercise. Glycogen is released from the muscles during exercise. This helps give fuel to the brain to keep your resolve strong for the day.

Glycogen is the body's source of sugar. It is stored in the muscles and in the liver. If there is a predator, the body stores enough glycogen (sugar energy) in the muscles so that you can run away quickly. When the glycogen is used up through consistent exercise, the liver sends out more glycogen to replenish the stores.

The brain also uses glycogen as a fuel. There is a part of the brain, if you are concentrating on a task or problem, that can deplete its glycogen stores. When the glycogen is depleted in this part of the brain, it makes you more impulsive. Here's the trick. If you don't exercise regularly, the liver is not in the habit of pumping out glycogen on a regular basis through exercise. There will be a delay of the needed supply of glycogen to the brain. This delay could decrease your resolve long enough for you to eat non-compliant foods.

What about Detoxification? How Bad Will It Be?

If you eat a diet that is high in processed foods, your body will want to eliminate the toxins as quickly as possible. The more toxic the diet, the stronger the detoxification symptoms.

I don't recall any serious detoxification symptoms but my diet was pretty clean before I started. Also, this is not like a cleanse. You are eating real food and lots of it. This will help in lessening the symptoms and their severity.

Detoxification symptoms are flu-like symptoms such as exhaustion, sweats, diarrhea, chills, and achiness. The good news is that these symptoms usually subside within a couple of days. Withdrawal symptoms can include irritability, crying jags, and insomnia. Cravings for foods, or substances, are common signs of withdrawal.

During this phase, you may feel irritable and nauseous, but you'll feel better after a few days. There are times that you might think you are becoming ill. But it is important to continue with the program. Do not take any medications to help with the withdrawal symptoms. The aim of cleaning up your diet is to flush the chemicals out of the body, not introduce more.

For a time, you may actually feel worse and may conclude that the program is not working. Yet, the symptoms are signs that the body is cleaning and repairing itself. This reaction is only temporary and usually lasts from one to three days.

Here are some coping strategies to help you manage the symptoms of detox:

1. Drink plenty of filtered water. Also, caffeine free herbal teas can help. Water especially helps if you are experiencing headaches. Chamomile tea is great if you are experiencing edginess and insomnia.

2. Herbs are diuretic. They allow your body to wash out waste products faster by urinating more. They support the lymphatic system's detoxifying abilities. They also strengthen the liver. The sample week's menu plan includes cilantro, parsley, turmeric and garlic. Which all support your detoxification.

3. If you are feeling tired or lethargic, this is your body's way of telling you to take a rest. This is another great thing about having all your meals ready to go. If you are tired you are minutes away from eating detox supporting foods.

4. Take hot showers or visit a sauna. You can sweat out toxins through your skin.

5. If you are emotional and are suffering from mood swings, meditate. Do some yoga or tai chi. Go for a walk preferably in nature. Some light exercise will help you feel better and more energized. Write in your journal or take a nap.

What Can I Drink?

When people ask this question, they want to hear good news about their bad habits as Dr. McDougall says. You can have as much filtered water as you can tolerate. You can drink caffeine-free herbal teas. A little lemon juice in water before meals helps to stimulate stomach HCl. Stomach acid (HCl) helps to break down your food. You cannot drink things that contain sugar. This includes alcohol which also lowers your resolve to be compliant. It is loaded with empty calories.

What About Coffee?

Nope. No coffee. The caffeine in coffee is a strong stimulant and makes it very difficult to sleep. It unnaturally ramps up your adrenaline. This makes you jittery and ready for flight or fight. Coffee is also an inflammatory substance. Do you have any inflammation in your body? Any aches and pains? You are contributing to the inflammation by continuing to drink coffee.

Caffeine withdrawal is one of the worst withdrawals related to food. If you are a serious coffee drinker, drinking more than 3 cups of coffee per day, you are strongly addicted. The withdrawal symptoms will be stronger and can last for days. If this is you, you are going to have to pick your battles. We are already changing your diet so you can continue to drink coffee for the first couple of weeks. (Obviously without cream or sugar or any fake substitutes.) Change your food first.

Then you can change to Fair Trade, organic decaffeinated beans and grind your own. Decaffeinated coffee has much less caffeine. But it is highly processed to extract the caffeine so this a temporary compromise.

Once you do this for a couple of weeks, you can try Dandy tea. Which is caffeine free but it comes in a powder and tastes like instant coffee. Or you can drink herbal teas.

The end goal is to be free from this addictive substance. Your energy levels will naturally increase. And you will no longer be dependent on caffeine to get you through your day. Your body will reward you with natural energy and you will sleep so much better.

What about Juicing?

No. Juicing is great way for people to get a lot of calories and nutrition into their bodies very quickly. Since all the pulp is removed and only the juice remains, your blood sugar will spike immediately. There is no fiber to slow it down. People who need to lose weight want to avoid blood sugar spikes at all costs.

Also, the calorie density increases tremendously. Can you eat a pound of apples in one sitting? A pound of apples (about 3 or 4 big ones) is around 300 calories. That's a lot of apples.

I could eat one or two and I would be full because of all the fiber. But those 3 or 4 apples juiced would barely make a dent in my hunger drive. I could drink three times that amount in juice before I even felt the least bit full. Compounded with the blood sugar spike, this could cause you to eat off plan. Personally, I can't afford to waste my calorie allotment on a small glass of juice. It won't fill me up and because of the blood sugar spike, I will feel like I am starving by the time I eat my next real meal.

What about Smoothies?

Again, no. Smoothies are a healthy way of maintaining or gaining weight. It's no way to lose weight. Even though the fiber is not removed, it is not intact. It has been pulverized down to a liquid form making it more calorie dense. It takes up less room in the stomach and it leaves the stomach much faster as the blender has done all the body's work for it. Conduct an experiment if you need proof. Put all the smoothie ingredients in a bowl in their intact form and eat it. You probably won't be able to eat it all before you are too full.

Also, people have a tendency to add little extras to their smoothies that they don't count towards their calories. Protein powders, plant milks, a little extra banana, some avocado, nuts and seeds. It is a slippery slope. Soon that innocent smoothie can have an extra 100 – 200 calories. It's not worth it.

What about Intermittent Fasting?

Ah! The latest thing. The aim of intermittent fasting is to shorten the feeding window, meaning when you eat, to about 8 hours a day and not to eat for 16 hours. The health benefits are many but mostly unsubstantiated. Intermittent fasting is good for weight loss. It also claims to boost metabolism a bit which is always a good thing.

Intermittent fasting helps you eat fewer calories because the feeding window is limited. We are already limiting our calories through the principles of calorie density. So, intermittent fasting isn't necessary to incorporate.

Intermittent fasting is not good for people who suffer from a binge eating disorder. Binge eaters eat large amounts of processed food within a short time window. If you have done this in the past, intermittent fasting is definitely not for you. It will make you reinforce old behaviors that got you to overeat in the first place.

I have found that on my journey my feeding window shortened after about a month. I found I had fewer cravings and ate less as well. Nothing was forced or planned or white knuckled. There was no willpower or clock watching necessary. If you want to try intermittent fasting, do it naturally. Listen to your body and follow your natural hunger drive.

My only suggestion is to allow three hours to pass after dinner before going to bed. This doesn't mean staying up until 3:00 am. Adjust your feeding window to suit your normal bedtime.

What about Supplementation?

I know all about supplementation. As a registered holistic nutritionist, I can tell you what are the best supplements for what ails you. I have taken tons of supplements to the point that I feared I would rattle when I walked. And the best quality ones can be very expensive. I could easily drop an extra $100 per month on vitamins, minerals, and probiotics.

Supplementation is very useful when you have a diagnosed condition. But by far the best way to get your vitamins and minerals is through food. That's what our bodies are designed to do. There is better absorption and assimilation of vitamins and minerals through food sources. There is one exception. Vitamin B12. Our bodies can't produce it and it is not readily found in food anymore. Vegans have always needed to supplement this but thanks to factory farming meat eaters need to as well.

B12 is a bacterium found in soil. When farm animals would eat grass or scratch in the dirt, they would ingest a little bit of soil. Their flesh would contain enough B12 that when people ate these animals, they would get their B12.

But due to factory farming, animals are no longer grazing and scratching for their food in the soil. They are fed grains in troughs. This means that not even meat eaters are getting enough B12. As plant eaters we have two options, eat our carrots fresh from the ground and dirty or take a B12 supplement.

So, what's the big fuss about B12? It is important for optimal functioning of the brain and nervous system. It is also important for the digestive, cardiovascular and immune systems. B12 also improves your energy levels, memory and mood.

Our diet is focused on the most nutrient dense foods available. But I recommend taking a B12 supplement as it is the only thing missing from our food.

As you continue to eat this way, not only will you lose the extra weight, you will feel your body getting healthier. All the fresh fruit and vegetables loaded with nutrition can replace a cupboard full of supplements. You will feel stronger and the little aches and pains will go away. If you give yourself enough time and patience you will feel energized and healthy. You won't want to go back to your old way of eating. Your body will respond to all the great nutrition it has been starving for all these years.

As a holistic nutritionist I must say that there is a need for supplementation. But only if you are dealing with a medical condition and can't resolve it with an optimal diet.

For example, many years ago, I was having problems with hypothyroidism. I lacked energy and the outer third of my eyebrows disappeared! My doctor threatened to put me on Synthroid. But I bought some time and treated myself with supplements. My thyroid markers in my blood work are within the normal range now. I know that my diligence with supplementation helped. But also, some small changes in my environment to avoid chemicals played an equally important role.

So, if you currently have a condition that you think supplements will resolve, wait. Give yourself the gift of three months on a clean diet. See if the condition will correct itself with excellent nutrition. If the condition does not improve, talk to a holistic nutritionist about supplementation.

You mentioned Spirulina. What's with That?

Yes, spirulina is great. As I mentioned it is algae. It stabilizes blood sugar so I can go a long time without getting hungry. It is high in protein. As a matter of fact, it is the highest vegan source of two important amino acids, glycine and proline. These amino acids together with vitamin C form the procollagen necessary for the body to make collagen. Collagen, as any aging woman knows, is what helps keep our skin looking young. It does more than that, though. Collagen is important for cartilage, bones, ligaments and tendons. So, if you want to keep your appetite at bay and keep your body young and healthy, use spirulina. With this diet you will get plenty of vitamin C daily through citrus fruits, berries and tomatoes.

What about Motivation?

Some people work well with an accountability partner. Me, not so much. Whenever I have tried to do anything with a buddy in the past, it hasn't seemed to work out in the long run. If you choose a friend to do it with you, you could end up sabotaging each other. Or become disappointed with the other person's lack of stick-to-itiveness. As far as going to the gym together, somehow you can't get your schedules to match. Dieting together can become an unhealthy competition or you could end up enabling each other to eat non-compliant foods. It could ruin your friendship.

The best thing that I have found for motivation is to emulate the people who have succeeded. They walk the talk every day. So rather than dragging along an unhealthy friend to the gym, or yoga class, or dance class, I make new friends there. These people are committed to their decision to get healthy and fit. If you want to be healthy and fit, make friends with people who are and learn from them.

It really helps to immerse yourself in the positive messages from the experts. When I started out, I felt very alone on my journey to my ideal weight. It's tough when you have a lot of weight to lose. Everyone who is near and dear to you either can't relate to your problems or aren't ready to change their lifestyle.

Also, as I mentioned before, you want to keep your mouth closed about your new way of eating. Wait until you have tried it for yourself and feel confident in the results. You don't want to be debating the merits of a nutrient dense diet before you even start. You want to make sure you have a firm footing in the lifestyle and get amazing results. Then you will be in a better position to convert others to your new way of eating. You will be speaking from personal experience rather than theory.

This is your journey. You can make it work for you. It worked for me. You can feel more connected to others who either teach the message or need support. Just like you. All this from the comfort of your home. Here's what I did:

1. I joined social media groups that support this lifestyle. Some groups are better a fit than others. You get to read some amazing weight loss stories. You get support with what you are dealing with almost immediately. You have a huge group of friends that will cheer for you when you reach even the smallest milestone. You can take part or simply read the posts of others going through the same process.

2. My environment is clean. So is my electronic environment. I stopped watching TV because some of the commercials or shows would trigger me. Instead, I watch health-related documentaries, webinars, and summits. You can find some on Netflix, PBS, Prime Video and YouTube. YouTube is especially good for finding lectures and videos with Dr. Doug Lisle and Chef AJ.

3. When I am cooking, I watch talks about calorie density and weight loss. Or I watch cooking demonstrations for plant based bulk cooking.

4. I listen to health-related podcasts and summits in my car.

5. I also read a lot. My top three reference books are:

- The Secrets to Ultimate Weight Loss by Chef AJ
- The McDougall Program for Maximum Weight Loss by Dr. John McDougall
- The Pleasure Trap by Dr. Doug Lisle and Dr. Alan Goldhamer

Printed in Great Britain
by Amazon